# Devotions
## for the
# ARMCHAIR
# QUARTERBACK

Score a touchdown
for the Lord!

Blessings
Jim

1 Con 2:9

Harley,
Hope you enjoy the
book. Your life has
been an inspiration to
me.

Blessings
Jim

# Devotions
## for the
# ARMCHAIR
# QUARTERBACK

## Jim Crosby

GOM LOGOS
An Imprint of Gom Publishing
Columbus, Ohio

**GOM LOGOS**

An Imprint of Gom Publishing
P.O. Box 211110, Columbus, Ohio 43221

Phone: 866.466.2608
Email: communications@gompublishing.com
Internet: **www.gompublishing.com**

Scripture quotations are taken from:

The Holy Bible, New International Version® (NIV). copyright ©1973, 1978, 1984 by International Bible Society. Used by permission of Zondervan. All rights reserved.

The Holy Bible, New Living Translation® (NLT), copyright ©1996. Used by permission of Tyndale House Publishers, Inc., Wheaton, Illinois 60189. All rights reserved.

The Holy Bible, King James Version (KJV).

ISBN: 1-932966-32-3 (previously ISBN: 1-932338-33-0)
Library of Congress Control Number: 2004108125

First Gom Logos printing: June 2004

Gom Logos™ and the Gom Logos logo are trademarks of Gom Publishing, LLC

# CONTENTS

*This book is dedicated to Bobby Bowden.*
*Florida State University's head coach who continues*
*to teach all of us how to win with class and grace*
*and to accept defeat with dignity.*

# ACKNOWLEDGEMENTS

**N**o one writes a book alone. It is usually when you've typed the last sentence that you truly realize how much help, encouragement, and support from others kept you going. It would not be possible to recognize everyone who influenced the writing of *Devotions for the Armchair Quarterback*. In some ways every football game I've watched and every Bible study, sermon, and Sunday school class I have experienced played a part in this book. However, there are some people without whose assistance this book would not have become a reality.

First, let me thank my wonderful brother and sister-in-law Bob and Mikki Crosby for their quality editing. This is a much better book because of their time and commitment to it. As with anything I do, this project was fueled by the prayers of Mom Crosby and our friend Dorothy Martin. I am also blessed to have two exceptional sons, Clint and Austin, whose tossing the football around with old Dad all these years helped inspire a lot of this book.

My radio friends at Clear Channel Worldwide played a big role. Chris Stuckey helped me refine many of these chapters in our weekly Monday Morning Devotion group. Thanks to Preston Scott (News Radio 1270, WFLA) who continues to set an example for us all on the radio and has supported my writing from day one. Steve and Sara (Magic 107.1, WTLY) for always being open to sharing the book with their loyal audience.

My church family at Killearn United Methodist Church continues to inspire me with their love of the Lord. Especially meaningful have been the sermons and friendship of pastors Bob Tindale, Bill Rhoads, and Betsy Ouellette. Thanks also to Herb McRae, Jim Hunt, and Ric Duggar, strong men of faith and superb book reviewers.

Judy and Rolla Carter of the Christian Bookstore are great friends who have contributed positive support and much needed sales promotion of my books. David Forister and Judy Menendez of the Lifeway Christian Store were among the first and most faithful in providing quality marketing and sales assistance.

Of utmost importance is the contribution of the one who influences and enriches every day of my life: the lovely Susette, my wife, who lovingly listened to every word of *Devotions for the Armchair Quarterback,* prayed for its success, and offered common-sense suggestions that enabled me to articulate the thoughts God sent my way about football and life.

—*Jim*

"For when that One Great Scorer comes to
mark against your name,
He writes—not that you won or lost—
but how you played the game."

Grantland Rice

# INTRODUCTION

The alarm clock jolts you into consciousness. It's Monday morning. As you struggle to get your bearings, a sense of melancholy rushes into your mind. You try to figure out why you feel bad. Then, you remember. Your favorite football team lost over the weekend. You were devastated.

Or perhaps this scenario greets your waking moments: The first coherent thoughts are happy ones. Real happy thoughts bordering on euphoria. Why do you feel so good? Oh yeah, your team won over the weekend. The swagger starts before your feet hit the floor.

It is amazing how the game of football impacts the moods, thoughts, and actions of its fans. That is what *Devotions for the Armchair Quarterback* is all about—dealing with the highs and lows, the joy and sadness, the ecstasy of winning, and the crushing blow of defeat.

*Devotions for the Armchair Quarterback* looks at the game of football from a scriptural perspective. The aim of this book is to help the die-hard fan keep victory in perspective and not "rub it in," and to deal with defeat and handle those depressing feelings that threaten to wreck your week.

The consequences of winning or losing football games as a mood influencer is not male specific. Women also seek a means of displacement for those rotten feelings that accompany defeat.

When your team loses, it is a natural reaction to place blame for the defeat on someone or a certain circumstance. Victory is so important that to not achieve it demands an explanation. Simple acceptance of a loss without comprehension of how it happened is not satisfactory. If you don't understand what caused defeat you're destined to lose again.

Although *Devotions for the Armchair Quarterback* is obviously directed toward football fans, the lessons learned from it may be applied to any sport. Wherever games are played there will always be a winner and a loser. How the outcome is dealt with reveals who the real winners and losers are.

Walter Alston, longtime manager of the Dodgers, once summed it up pretty good when he said, "Sure you feel better and you sleep better when you win. But, there's nothing you can do about a game that is over. You can't change it. You can replay it as many times as you want, but the score is always the same. All you can do is learn from it and look ahead to tomorrow."[1]

When they lose a game, the coaches and players subject themselves to a lot of self-examination and recriminations while trying to learn from their mistakes and looking ahead. *Devotions for the Armchair Quarterback* enhances a fan's understanding of this. By reading about each aspect of the game and applying Biblical principles to them, you will achieve an understanding and appreciation of football that transcends wins and losses.

Happy reading and may the outcomes you encounter be more joy-tempering than sadness-buffering. Maybe the best team doesn't always win, but those who best deal with the result are the true winners.

## Chapter One
# THE GAME PLAN

*For I know the plans I have for you, declares the Lord.*
*Plans to prosper you, not to harm you.*
*Plans to give you hope and a future.*

Jeremiah 29:11

I t all starts with a game plan! From the first kickoff in August through the NCAA's Championship Game and the NFL's Super Bowl in January, football fans live and die with the fortunes of their favorite teams.

On a Monday Morning after your team wins, somehow the world feels like a better place. You're invincible, maybe even cocky. But if your team lost over the weekend, there's a tendency to start the week feeling down. Sometimes it's hard to put it all in perspective. After all, football is just a game!

But, as football coaches are fond of telling the players, there are lessons learned in playing football that can better equip the player to handle the vagaries of life. Likewise, there are lessons for football fans that also equate to successfully handling life's ups and downs.

All fans are familiar with the term "game plan." It's a phrase that has become so commonplace it permeates our conversations in many areas. No football team could hope to win or would even dare to try approaching a game without a game plan. Nowadays with everything on computer, coaches are able to compile an exceptional amount of information about their opponents and about their own team.

The defensive coaches have a printout of all the tendencies of the opponent on offense. Before they even kick off they know what their opponent is likely to do when they have the ball on their own 40-yard line with third down and four yards for a first down. At a glance, the defensive coordinator can scan the chart and discover on what percentage of plays from that field position his opponent has called a running play and how often they call a pass. Then, he signals the captain on the field a defensive alignment that should negate the play.

At the same time, the offensive staff must know what patterns they have fallen into on third-and-four from the forty since the defensive coaches can anticipate the play based on prior tendencies. It becomes quite a guessing game with a lot of other variables factored in such as; which players are fresh at the time, how the game plan is working to that point, and any surprises the opponents have come up with. It's a matter of continually adjusting within the scope of the entire game plan to determine what will work best at the moment.

Sometimes the other team comes out with radical alignments…changes not seen in any of the videos of other games. Then your game plan, the one you felt so good about formulating during a week of practice and planning sessions, becomes practically worthless. Maybe you have a great passing game and the other team decides to focus on the concept of stopping the pass, completely disdaining the threat of the running game. If they drop eight or nine players back in coverage and rush two, they are daring you to run the ball. The offensive coaches can be hard-headed and stick to the plan they so painstakingly crafted, possibly losing the game, or they can adjust to the circumstances, run the ball and try to force the defense to abandon the strategy.

So it is in life. As our scripture today tells us, God has a plan for each of our lives. It is a plan that will enable us to prosper. If all the other variables we encounter in our daily lives are constant and we deal with them within God's will, then everything will be fine. The game plan will work and we'll win out with no problem.

But, how many days can you remember in your life where everything went as expected? Any? Probably not! If it was just between us and God, it would be a lot easier. Then it would just be "trust and obey." But, there is the human factor. All these other folks, equipped with a free will, too, come into our lives with unexpected actions and force us out of our game plan. We must get out of our comfort zone. We have to go to a strategy we don't consider to be the optimum choice.

Sometimes we get so far afield we wonder what happened to the game plan we thought God had for our lives. That's the time to go to God in prayer and ask where you are headed. Are you going in the right direction? If you are not still on target to achieve that dream, maybe it was your game plan, but not God's. It didn't have his stamp of approval. Ask Him for a plan. Ask Him to give you the wisdom to discern what His plan is and how to execute it. But, don't give up too easily on your dreams.

Kurt Warner, two-time NFL Player of the Year and Super Bowl winning QB for the St. Louis Rams, had a dream to play professional football. But, none of the big colleges wanted him, so he played Division 1-AAA ball for the University of Northern Iowa. Then, after college, no NFL team courted him so he played Arena League Football. Next, he hooked on with a team in the NFL-European League.

After playing overseas for a season, Warner tried out and became the second string QB for the Rams. In his book, *All Things Possible*,[2] Warner recalls those days and says, "I could roam the aisles of my local supermarket and be recognized by absolutely no one. Heck, only five years earlier, I worked at a supermarket stocking shelves on the graveyard shift for minimum wage at the Hyvee, in Cedar Falls, Iowa."

Two hundred and fifty-six pages after that statement in the same book,[3] he has recounted his miraculous climb to the top echelon of the National Football League as a Super Bowl winning QB, a status many of the all-time great QBs, never achieved, and he makes this statement. "It would have been easy to feel sorry for myself or to become bitter and walk away. But, if I have done anything by beating the odds, I hope it's that I've spread a positive message to people who otherwise might not be listening. I view my struggle as analogous to that of David against Goliath. David was a guy nobody ever gave a chance, a man who came out of nowhere to display an incredible amount of power and control. He couldn't have slain Goliath without an unyielding faith in God, and he wasn't trying to help himself, he was also working to uplift his people." God rearranged Kurt Warner's plans a number of times and blessed his faithfulness beyond even his fondest dreams.

In football there are plans within a plan. The master plan for the team is based on many factors. The overall scheme might be to implement a passing attack. Within that general plan the emphasis might be placed on passing. They will plan to pass 60% of the time and run the other 40%. That would be the mindset each week as the game plan is put together. But, say the opponent you are playing is ranked first in pass defense and is giving up less than 100 yards a game through the air. Conversely, their opponents are gaining over 300 yards, on average, by rushing against them. Maybe your running game hasn't been so hot. The difficulty in drafting a plan for that game concerns whether you should challenge their defensive strength with your offensive strength, or go with the offensive aspect you don't execute as well, thereby taking advantage of their weakness against the run.

It may sometimes seem that God's game plan is taking a beating in your life, just as the game plan of your favorite team sometimes gets thrown off-track. You may feel like every time you plan to do something that the circumstances are stacked against you. But, the way to succeed, even when the odds are against you, is to stay strong in the faith like Kurt Warner did. Keep seeking his help, refining the plan as circumstances warrant and as He directs you. Then, miraculously, you'll see your life start changing as you begin doing the things that are in His will... taking the corrective measures and making adjustments that put you on the right course.

If your team lost its last game, it probably was not because of a faulty or short-sighted game plan by the coaching staff. More likely it was a case of inferior execution of the plan by the players or simply superior execution by the opponents of their plan. Or maybe they just got outplayed.

As Bruce Wilkinson points out in his landmark book, *The Prayer of Jabez*.[4] God delights in blessing you and has even greater things in store than you would think to ask for. The way to be on a winning track is to make sure you understand your heavenly Father's plan and to execute it properly. It is a plan that won't get outplayed by His enemies. God's Game Plan cannot be defeated!

## Prayer for Guidance

Lord, we know you have a plan for everything. You created the universe according to a master plan. You created each one of us within that plan and you have a game plan for our lives. We pray for your daily guidance that we might understand all aspects of your plan and that we might execute to perfection this blue-print for our lives. May our thoughts and actions be pleasing to you!

Amen!

# Chapter Two

# THE COACHES

> *And even when you do ask, you don't get it*
> *because your whole motive is wrong,*
> *you want only what will give you pleasure.*
>
> **James 4:3**

**F**lorida State University Coach Bobby Bowden was asked at a prayer breakfast in Fort Lauderdale, Florida if he ever prayed for the opposing team. "Oh sure, I'll pray for our opponents," he said with a serious look on his face, then he added with an impish grin. "Any time we're a 50 or 60 point favorite, I'll pray for our opponent."

Bowden, who started his current run at FSU in 1976, is living proof that good coaching makes a big difference. He took over a Florida State team that had only won a total of four games the previous three seasons. In two years, he had jumped the record to 10–2 and has not had a losing season since that first year. His 330 victories rank him second all-time among all NCAA Division 1-A coaches.

Coach Bowden holds a daily devotion with his coaches before each staff meeting. He also leads his team in prayer before they run through the goal posts to begin a game. He often asks God in his prayers to grant specific requests.

But does he ever pray for a win? No! Never! "I start each coaching session with Bible reading, devotion, and prayer," said Bowden. "I tell our coaches, I want to use it as a time to ask God to give us guidance. I don't believe God's going to make us win. I don't pray for a win. We know every coach in the country wants to win. We know everybody wants to win. But, we just ask Him to give us wisdom in decisions we have to make. And to show us how to teach our boys to do their best and things like that."[5]

Winning is something Don Shula is very familiar with. The former Miami Dolphin mentor is the only coach in NFL history to record a perfect season: 17 wins, no losses. If any coach ever deserved to feel he was "hot stuff," it would be Shula. However, in his book, *Everyone's a Coach*, written with Ken Blanchard, defines Ego as "Edging God Out." He writes, "Great coaches are not consumed by their own importance. When they win they are happy. When they lose they are not happy."

Once when the Dolphins were losing and Shula was very unhappy, he lost his temper on national television. Even worse was the fact that an open microphone picked up his taking of the Lord's name in vein. When he was flooded with letters concerning his behavior, Shula took time to answer every letter personally. He apologized to each person without offering excuses and stated that he valued the letter writer's respect. He said he would do his best thereafter to earn the respect back.[6]

8

Most successful coaches succeed because they are adept at "coaching the coaches." The key is to get a good staff in place and let them do their jobs. However, the overall plan and organization rests on the shoulders of the head coach. They come together as a staff and discuss the scheme of things, then the assistant coaches teach the players how to execute the plan. Coaches who don't win don't stay around that long. These days owners and school presidents have itchy trigger fingers because the pressure is on them to have a winning program. So, coaches don't usually enjoy the leisure of having a "five-year plan" or one that is longer.

As coach Joe Gibbs, winner of two Super Bowls with the Washington Redskins, says, "You win games by scoring more points than the other guys, but you can lose in a whole lot of ways."[7] Losing a game because you didn't have all the eventualities covered is one of the biggest fears coaches have. So, what areas to concentrate on and how much time to devote to each are some of the biggest decisions a coaching staff faces.

In our daily lives we face constant temptations that can cause us to lose out on achieving our goals. Coaches talk a lot about not losing focus. When you're in a deep hole, backed up near your goal line and a hostile crowd has elevated the noise to an ear-splitting level, it is easy to lose focus.

Likewise, when a deadline is approaching us and everything goes wrong—the fax machine runs out of paper, an electrical storm knocks out the phone line and even worse, the internet—it is easy to throw up your hands and cave in to the pressure.

This is a good time to remember the words in **Hebrews 12:1-2.** *Therefore since we are surrounded by such a huge crowd of witnesses to the life of faith, let us strip off every weight that slows us* *down, especially the sin that so easily hinders our progress. We do this by keeping our eyes on Jesus, on whom our faith depends from start to finish.*

The lessons learned in church sound so right and logical—on Sunday. But on Monday, outside the sanctuary, in front of that "crowd of witnesses," it is sometimes difficult to stay the course. We know the right way to go, but these distractions threaten to knock us off course. The way to stay on course is to pray constantly, asking for the things that will best allow us to use our talents for God's glory, not our own.

Likewise, the coach of your favorite team must stick to what he believes in when the going gets rough. Coaches like Bobby Bowden, Don Shula, Joe Gibbs, and other Christian coaches have a foundation of faith that enables them to keep their eye on the ultimate prize. They provide good examples for us to use in our daily battles.

On July 27, 1996, Joe Gibbs was inducted into the Pro Football Hall of Fame. Here's what he said about the honor. "The answer is that God picks very average men and women, and what he does is give them a life, some talent, and surround them with great people."

The way to gain honors that count for something is to honor God with the things you do.

## Prayer for Guidance

Lord, we know that we are the coach of our own team. We don't operate in isolation because others are always observing what we do. We understand that there are many negative obstacles that make us lose focus in our lives. As Christians, we are scrutinized closely. But, because of our faith, we know that we cannot be ultimately defeated. As long as we ask you for guidance and do not ask amiss, for selfish purposes, we'll coach our team to the victory we have in Jesus.

Amen

## Chapter Three
# THE QUARTERBACK

*Much is required from those to whom much is given,*
*and much more is required from those*
*to whom much more is given.*

Luke 12:48

**W**hen my son Austin was growing up, he played in a flag football league for nine and ten-year-olds. Although he was the best wide receiver on the team, none of the other players could accurately get the ball to him with their passes. Since Austin was also a good passer, he was moved to quarterback.

Soon after the switch, I noticed that the team was taking an unusual amount of time in the huddle before running their plays. Later I asked Austin why. He said, "Well, Dad, I have to tell each player what to do on the play." As the quarterback he not only had to know what his job was on the play, but every other position player as well. And at that age a lot of the other players couldn't remember their responsibility on the plays that were called and had to be reminded.

Although quarterbacks get most of the credit when things go right, they earn it. For the quarterback to successfully execute a play, he has to know where all his players are going to be on the field. Likewise, he must anticipate where all of the defenders are going to be, especially on a pass play, so he doesn't throw it to the wrong place.

I remember once while playing the running back position, the QB called for a direct snap to me. I was supposed to throw the ball to the open receiver down field. But, when I looked down field all I could see was a bunch of bodies, and I found it difficult to pick out one of my players. Consequently, I threw an interception. And that was with little defensive pressure on me.

In today's game of football the quarterback is asked to stand his ground, ignore the fact that two 300-pound defensive linemen are coming at him full throttle, pick out his receiver and make a perfect throw. It ain't easy. It takes concentration, vision, agility, accuracy, and most of all—courage.

At Florida State University, Danny Kanell found himself in the enviable position of being the starting quarterback, but the unenviable situation of having to replace Heisman Trophy winner Charlie Ward. Then came a time when Kanell bottomed out. He could have given up, but instead he played 12 minutes of football that college fans, especially Seminoles, will remember forever.

FSU found itself trailing their bitter rivals Florida by 24–3 at halftime. As they left for the locker room, the boos came cascading down from the home fans in their own stadium. "I felt like everybody was against me. The fans didn't want to see me out there. Then, I thought about how many Christian friends and my family were praying for me. That really uplifted me and gave me the strength I needed," said Kanell.[8]

Things got worse before they got better. The Gators scored again in the third quarter to give them a 31–3 lead. Then Kanell spearheaded one of the most amazing comebacks in college football history. In the final 12 minutes, the Seminoles scored 28 points to pull a tie game out of the face of certain defeat. In the final quarter, Kanell completed 18 of 22 passes for 232 yards. The power of prayer gave him confidence and his entire career turned around.

Courage and daring are part of the game for the signal caller. In the 1971 AFC championship game Miami Dolphin QB Bob Griese took a vicious hit from Baltimore Colt linebacker Jack Curtis, which drew a 15-yard personal foul penalty. The hit made things a little bit hazy for Griese. But, shaking it off on a third-and-two situation, Griese faked a handoff to Larry Csonka and hit Paul Warfield with a pass to the five-yard line that turned the game around.

After the 21–0 victory over Johnny Unitas and company, Coach Don Shula said, "That was a guts call. Griese called it, not me. It's one of the things I like most about Griese. He isn't afraid to take things into his own hands on a risky play. It's harder to do that than just handing off to a guy and thinking, 'I hope he makes it.' That's what gives a team confidence in its quarterback."[9]

There is a place in everyone's life for risk-taking. There is a time to play it safe. Knowing when the time is ripe to go-for-broke isn't easy because part of the role in leading lies also in knowing when to show restraint. Among Jesus' disciples, Peter was the quarterback. He was confident and aggressive.

Sometimes Peter was too aggressive—like when he pulled out his sword and cut off the ear of a high priest's servant when the soldiers came to arrest Jesus. Jesus spent a lot time teaching Peter restraint. Peter learned his lessons well and would later write in **1 Peter 2: 13,15** *Therefore submit yourselves to every ordinance of man for the Lord's sake...For this is the will of God that by doing good you may put to silence the ignorance of foolish men.*

By his impetuous action Peter could have compromised the entire mission of Jesus. They were badly outnumbered by the soldiers. An all-out battle with a lot of bloodshed could have ensued, but Jesus avoided it by calmly reattaching the man's ear. Sometimes a coach must calm down his leader to get the game back under control, especially in hostile territory

But, as it says in **2 Timothy 1:7,** *For God has not given us a spirit of fear and timidity, but of power, love, and self-discipline.* We are to boldly go forth, confident that we are on God's Squad. With His coaching, our decision making ability, and our talents, we will win out.

Bill Hinson was an All-Southwestern Conference quarterback at Baylor who later went to seminary and became pastor of First Baptist Church in Ft. Lauderdale. When the Baltimore Colts played the New York Jets in the 1969 Super Bowl in Miami, Pastor Hinson put a sign out in front of the church on a busy street that said: "Football is not mentioned in the Bible. Nevertheless, Yea Colts!"

However, the pastor's preference was overcome when a quarterback named Joe Namath, imitating the spirit of boldness described in **2 Timothy** shockingly "guaranteed" in public the upstart Jets would beat the well-established Colts. Then, Namath made the prediction come true by playing a solid, focused, nearly flawless game.

The Lord has given much to each of us. Therefore, he expects much in return. He has more than a "passing" interest in the way we quarterback our lives. He has guaranteed the victory. We just have to play the game His way to win.

## Prayer for Guidance

Lord, you have given each of us talents far beyond those that we use daily in our lives. Victory in Christ is guaranteed. But, sometimes we are impetuous and get out of control in our haste to accomplish things in our lives. We rush ahead and don't use those talents in the right way. Give us the wisdom to know when to boldly take a risk and when to wait. Help us to quarterback our own lives in a way that will be pleasing to you and lead us along the path of righteousness in your name.

Amen!

## Chapter Four
# THE OFFENSE

> *Watch out that you do not lose what you have worked for,*
> *but that you may be rewarded fully.*
>
> 2 John 8

**A**t Picture Day on college campuses throughout America, there are no losers. All decked out in their clean, shiny uniforms with not even a grass stain to be seen, everybody looks like an All-American. Of course, nobody has even gotten hit yet—not by their own teammates in practice nor an opponent in a game.

Throughout the summer most of these players have worked out, stayed in shape, and come back in peak condition. They'll begin the arduous "two-a-days," then hold scrimmages, then taper off to get their "legs back."

Invariably, at this point someone will say, "We're ready to play somebody. We want to play a game. We're tired of hitting each other." By this point most of the offense is in. Those bread and butter plays that will carry the offense through the season have been practiced and practiced ad nauseam.

Remembering the lessons learned during those hot August days, staying focused and not letting them get away is the goal as the season gets underway. Teams don't want all that toiling under the broiling, summer sun to have been for naught. As the scripture says, "Watch out that you do not lose what you have worked for…" Losing focus for a play, quarter, or game can start a downward slide that will negate the overall goal—to win a championship. Everybody wants to do that. Only one team will!

But until you play a game, you won't know what that offense can do. As the legendary Bear Bryant once said, "You never know how a horse will pull until you hook him to a heavy load."[10]

It takes 11 committed players who are in sync and have achieved a special, coordinated, offensive rhythm to get the ball into the end zone. Touchdowns are the lifeblood of the offense. They keep the offensive heartbeat strong.

Field goals are okay. But, a team settles for a field goal when it can't score a touchdown. On the other hand, scoring a TD provides a very positive boost for an offense. It is a team effort because it takes good blocking, deceptive fakes, precise pass patterns, or quick hitting (of the holes), and on-target throws or crisp hand-offs.

The defense bows it neck and tries to stop the offensive juggernaut. So, when the offense breaks through the battle lines and into the end zone it is a success for the offense and failure by the defense.

It takes hard work to score touchdowns. They don't just happen. An offensive unit must practice a play hundreds of times to get it down in a game. As the late Vince Lombardi once said, "The dictionary is the only place where success comes before work. Hard work is the price we must all pay for success." [11]

In the 1993 AFC Playoffs the Houston Oilers took their eyes briefly off the prize. Who could blame them? Warren Moon had the Oiler offense humming like, uh, a well-oiled machine. Houston ran up a 28–3 lead by halftime, while the Buffalo offense behind substitute QB Frank Reich accomplished nothing.

When Houston increased its lead to 32 points in the third quarter, all hope seemed lost for the Bills. But Frank Reich had faith. In college at Maryland, he had brought his team back from a 31-point deficit to a 42–40 victory over the Miami Hurricanes. As he looked at the scoreboard he paused to remember and gain a positive affirmation from that incredible collegiate achievement. Then, giving his fingers a quick lick to moisten them, he tightened his chin strap and went to work.

The flurry of Bills touchdowns aided by recovered on-side kicks and superb defense catapulted them into the lead, 38–35 with still 3:08 left to play. Behind Reich they had made an improbable comeback and would eventually win the game in overtime, 41–38. Reich credits God's grace, not his own talents, for that comeback and the other things he achieves in life.

"I like the often-use acronym G. R. A. C. E.—God's Riches at Christ's Expense," says Reich, who explains the difference between grace and mercy as, "Grace is receiving something that we do not deserve while mercy is not receiving what we do deserve."

Too often in life we feel the way Frank Reich did before his conversion. He viewed religion as another game, one at which he wasn't playing his best, but was doing okay. "I was convinced that God graded on a curve," he said. He felt certain he was above the curve. Then, he says, "My world was rocked when I found out God doesn't grade on a curve. He requires a score of 100% to get into heaven."

Then, Reich got worried. But through God's grace he was directed to **2 Ephesians 5:21.** *God made Him who had no sin to be sin for us, so that in Him we might become the righteousness of God.* Then Reich realized that Jesus had already scored 100% on the test. All Frank had to do was place his faith in Jesus and he was "credited with His righteousness, while Jesus was credited with Reich's sin."

To have a 32 point lead and lose a game, or to have the best record in football and get beaten in the playoffs, losing the reward a team has worked so hard for, is tragic. But to live a full life on earth and lose the reward of salvation in the end because other things superseded a faith in Jesus Christ is the ultimate tragedy.

### Prayer for Guidance

Lord, we are caught up in the pursuit of daily goals and achieving short-term, earthly success. We work hard to perfect our performance and enjoy a life we deem worth living. We enjoy your blessings and take them for granted. Help us not to lose the ultimate reward, the only one worth seeking—eternal life through faith in Jesus Christ.

Amen!

## Chapter Five

# THE DEFENSE

> *Be strong and courageous. Do not be terrified;*
> *do not be discouraged, for the Lord your God*
> *will be with you wherever you go.*
>
> Joshua 1:9

**"D**ee-fense! Dee-fense! Dee-fense!" How many times have you heard that cheer of encouragement go up from the fans in the stands? Many times!

How many times have you heard the chant—Offense! Offense! Offense! None, probably. Why is that? It takes good offensive play as well as good defensive play to win football games. Fans usually know more about offense than they do defense. Scoring touchdowns wins games. But, keeping teams from scoring touchdowns may be even more important. So why more "defense–specific" cheering than for the offense?

Robert Neyland, who earned the rank of General in World War II and then built a powerhouse at the University of Tennessee, became a legend in the coaching ranks. His philosophy is still widespread in the game because what he said made sense. His planning started with this premise: "Football is a game of defense and field position." [12] The defense tries to set up touchdowns by providing good field position for the offense.

Offensive players seem to get more recognition than defensive players. A prime example is the 1972 Miami Dolphins who recorded a perfect 17–0 record. The offensive players such as Bob Griese, Jim Kiick, Larry Csonka, and Paul Warfield became household names. While the lesser known defensive stars, Nick Buonoconti, Dick Anderson, Bob Baumhower, Bill Stanfil, and Jake Scott were virtual unknowns. To counter balance this lack of publicity, the Dolphin Defenders named themselves "the no-name defense." The ploy worked and attracted a lot of attention to the excellence of Miami's defensive contributions.

Sometimes the defense will earn recognition, but a certain portion of the defense will get more credit than the rest. The 1964 Florida State Seminoles, while compiling a 9–1–1 record behind a wide-open, throw-it-from-anywhere offense under Bill Peterson, also played strong defense. To show camaraderie, the defensive line and linebackers shaved their heads and called themselves "The Seven Magnificents." It was a take-off on the Yul Brynner moved "The Magnificent Seven." When they started to attract a lot of attention, the Seminole Secondary began to refer to itself as the "Forgotten Four." But, the entire Seminole defense was becoming well-known to the fans.

The game of football seems to go through stages. Sometimes offenses are ahead of defenses overall. Some new offensive scheme is unveiled and a lot of teams pick up on it and start using it while defenses try to figure out how to stop it. Some past examples of offensive innovation include the Single-Wing, T-Formation, Split-T, I-Formation, Wishbone, Pro Set, and West Coast Offense. All of these have had their day. To counteract them new defensive alignments have sprung up going from a Six-Man Line, to a 4–3, a 3–4, Nickel Defense, Dime Defense, Prevent Defense, or a combination of all. The offensive and defensive minds are always trying to out-strategize each other.

In the 1999 regular season the St. Louis Rams, behind Kurt Warner, passed for 4,353 yards and 41 touchdowns. They added 1,063 more passing yards in the post-season and set a record with 414 yards passing in the Super Bowl victory over Tennessee. Everyone was talking about the Rams offense as they dominated all the NFC defenses.

But, the very next season The Baltimore Ravens swung the pendulum back to the defensive side. After the Ravens' Super Bowl victory people were saying they might have the best defense ever as they dethroned the Rams. Linebacker Peter Boulware said, "I think if we scored 10 points our offense would be accused of running up the score. I think we went four or five games where we didn't score a touchdown."[13] Defense had won a championship for the Rams and now relegated to the history books was the impressive offensive explosion of the Rams in 1999.

While the offense is charged with taking territory, the defense has the responsibility of defending it. As offenses get more complex and sophisticated, defenders must counteract that by raising their level of performance. When the Rams won the Super Bowl they were said to have over 700 plays in their playbook. Defending against that much offensive ingenuity takes a totally focused defense.

Defending against Satan's playbook in our daily lives takes a focused effort on our part. The minute we let down he slips right in the seam of our zone defense and scores his points. Boulware says he found the key to success on and off the field is prayer. "Prayer is like breathing to me. It is the key to life—talking to the Lord. It's not only me praying, but I have a lot of people praying for me, and I pray for other people."

The hallmark of a good defense is endurance. In life you will encounter unexpected situations that require you to adjust and think on your feet. You may not have the proper defense set up for it. Evil may have made inroads into your territory before you had a proper defense set up. Even though you aren't fully prepared, you have to buckle up that helmet and defend anyway. The battle can often be long and hard. Endurance is called for!

Problems strike us when least expected. They put you in the kind of position similar to the football situation in which the QB throws an interception that is returned deep in his team's territory. The defense must rush onto the field, often with their backs to the goal line and provide damage control. The advantage is fully with the offense because by setting up shop in the enemy's territory they can be more creative. They are free from the fear of giving up the ball near their own goal line.

So it is with Satan's inroads. If one of his ploys causes you to lose focus and take your eyes off the Lord, he'll get even trickier. Soon you're trying to plug so many holes, the task seems impossible. You defend the run when it's a pass. Then he runs all over your pass defense. You're so busy trying to do it all on your own, you've forgotten to pray for help. Like Peter Boulware said, "the key is prayer." That's your main defense.

When you pray, you don't have to try to be a one-man team. You receive help from three pretty good players—the Heavenly Father, His Son, and the Holy Spirit. They are always on call. As one anonymous writer once said, "Give your problems to God, He's going to be up all night anyway." Prayer is one of the best defensive strategies you can use. When prayer becomes like breathing, peace replaces worries.

God's defensive strategies have stood the test of time. Prayer, Bible study, and faith can defend against any offense.

## Prayer for Guidance

Lord, sometimes we feel like we are always on the defensive side of things. Problems bombard us, evil tempts us, and we appear to be losing the battle. Help us to remember the strategies you have given us to use. Remind us to commit all things to you in prayer, being confident that you will help us to defend ourselves successfully then go on the offensive attack as we move forward in your name.

Amen!

## Chapter Six

# THE RECEIVERS

> *God arms me with strength; he has made my way safe.*
> *He makes me surefooted as a deer, leading me safely*
> *along mountain heights.*
>
> Psalm 18:32-33

**T**he excitement level rises as the fans sitting high in the stands, with a panoramic view of the field, can see the wide receiver streaking down the far sidelines. Then as those who had been watching the quarterback become aware of what is happening, they rise to their feet.

As a defensive end bears down on the QB, he cocks his arm and releases the ball. The oval shaped pigskin sails into the air. The drama continues. Will the ball make it to the speedy receiver? As a defender closes in, the ball settles over his shoulder and into the hands of the receiver. The radio announcer shouts, "He's at the 15, the 10, the 5, Touchdown!"

The long bomb is the most exciting play in football. It takes great skill, concentration, and timing on the part of the quarterback.

Unless the receiver catches the ball, nothing happens. Receivers come in all shapes and sizes. There are fast receivers, quick receivers, shifty receivers who can fake and cut, and those with great jumping ability who can leap high above defenders. Not all receivers possess all of those attributes. But, to be successful there is one thing they all must have—good hands.

A good example is Fred Biletnikoff of the Oakland Raiders. He did not have great speed. But because of his great hands and quick moves, he was able to play 15 years in the NFL, with the same team, and caught 589 passes with 76 of them going for touchdowns. Biletnikoff set records because he didn't drop passes.

One of the original "good hands" people was a tall skinny end from the University of Alabama by the name of Don Hutson. He became a member of the Green Bay Packers in 1935. On his very first play he caught an 83-yard touchdown pass. Up to this point running the ball had been the offensive strategy of choice. But with the Packers gobbling up yardage and scoring through the air, the passing game had arrived and the sure-handed receivers (called ends back then) became a valuable commodity.

Hutson led the league in receiving eight times. In 1942 he became the first pass-catcher to amass more than 1,000 receiving yards in a season when he totaled 1,211 yards and scored 17 touchdowns. Hutson established a long-standing record by catching a pass in 95 consecutive games.[14] He was the antithesis of the Biblical scripture that "it is more blessed to give than to receive." However, by receiving he was actually "giving" to his team because the passes he caught validated the Packers' offensive strategy.

Before a receiver ever goes out for a pass in a game he has caught hundreds of balls in practice. Each step has been measured.

He knows that when he has gone 10 yards he should look for the ball to be delivered by the quarterback. Or maybe he must go 15 yards, cut to the sidelines, and as he makes his cut the ball will be there. As the legendary coach Pop Warner once said, "You play the way you practice."[15]

Still, it's different when it's game time. The receiver doesn't just run a perfect pattern, get hit with a perfect pass, and score. There's a little matter of the defense to contend with and a bunch of hard-hitting defenders in the secondary who make it difficult.

There are also a variety of defensive tactics a receiver must overcome to have a chance to catch a pass. Sometimes he gets hit at the line of scrimmage and knocked off course, or he may be double-teamed, zoned, or held (if the refs aren't looking). There are any number of defensive strategies he must out-maneuver to get open. Nobody lets him just run out there and catch a pass like he did in practice.

Our daily tasks unfold much like those of a receiver. Just as it takes ingenuity and patience for the receiver to be successful, so it is with the Christian in daily life. We learn great lessons from the life of Christ when we read the Bible and attend church. But, there are all kinds of temptations, tests, trials, and roadblocks in life that cause us to get knocked out of the pattern we had hoped to run. The road to success is seldom straight and is usually filled with potholes.

If a receiver knows the QB is expecting him to arrive at a certain spot where the ball will be delivered, he must make an all out effort to get there or the pass will not be completed. It takes determination, ingenuity, and sometimes physical strength to fight off or outsmart the DB and make it happen.

As Christians we must be determined to follow those lessons learned from our Bible study. When bad things happen that threaten to knock us off course we need to use what Pastor Rick Warren of Saddleback Church in California calls the "principle of replacement."[16] Warren proposes that when temptation strikes we take the advice found in **Romans 12:21** and replace evil with good. We replace those evil thoughts with good thoughts. "You defeat bad thoughts by thinking something better." Satan's double-team, bump-and-run, or zone defense is defeated as we move into an area where he is vulnerable the area of right-thinking and righteous actions.

Sometimes we keep trying to beat the coverage with the same self-defeating strategy. Satan might give us room. We attend church, study God's word, and get all that good training. But Satan uses the wily cornerback's strategy, who gives ground to make the receiver think he is open, then quickly closes the open area as the ball is thrown and intercepts the pass. Satan takes away our opportunity to score one for Jesus Christ. He tempts us and make us think we are "open"—what we are doing is good. When, really, it is deceivingly contrary to what we have learned in church and Bible study. It will not score a touchdown in our lives. Too late we come up empty handed, realize Satan has deceived us, and the sure scoring play has become an interception. The strategy has backfired on us. The evil one has stolen our joy.

Irving Fryar was an All-American receiver at Nebraska who was drafted by the Patriots. He quickly began to mess up his promising career through drug usage. Eventually, on an October night when a brawl started in a night club, Fryar was hit over the head with a baseball bat and knocked cold. When the police arrived and found a gun in his boot, they arrested him.

Having hit bottom Fryar found himself in a church where he made the biggest reception of this life. "I had to give up and go up front and confess my sins and give my life to Christ," he said. The change in his life was astounding as he became a preacher off the field. On the field the honors and Pro Bowl invitations started to come his way. Irving Fryar had replaced evil with good in his life.

Consider this replacement theory when things go awry in your life. Then, you will "receive" more blessings from God than you had thought possible.

## Prayer for Guidance

Lord, we want to receive your blessings, but sometimes we follow a self-defeating strategy. We follow the temptations that waylay your plans for us. We practice Biblical principles, but in the game of life we don't execute them because it looks different out there. Satan's coverages are often disguised to look like an easy score for us, when the opposite is true. Lord, help us to discern real opportunities from unreal ones and follow the strategies in life that will be pleasing to you and ensure success.

Amen.

## Chapter Seven
# THE LINEBACKERS

*Praise be to the Lord my Rock, who trains my hands for war, my fingers for battle. He is my loving God and my fortress, my stronghold and my deliverer, my shield, in whom I take refuge, who subdues peoples under me.*

Psalm 144: 1-2

**R**ugged individualists—an apt description for linebackers. They must be strong, quick, and football smart. Linebackers, in the words of the late, great Florida A&M coach Jake Gaither, need to be "agile, mobile, and hostile." Some are flat-out mean!

When you think of the great linebackers, names that immediately come to mind include Dick Butkus, Ray Nitsche, Mike Singletary, and more recent great ones such as Nick Buonoconti and Derrick Brooks. Each one of these hard-nosed players had the ability to sniff out a play and arrive at the spot where the ball was headed, then try to take the ball carrier's head off.

Ever meet a person who always had an angle, no matter what the subject? The angle he or she had was usually different from the approach any other folks would take to achieve their goals. Well, a linebacker is a guy with an angle. In fact, angles are very important for the linebacker, who ordinarily lines up anywhere from a few steps to a few yards behind the defensive lineman.

What the linebacker is looking for is the best angle to take so he will get to the guy with the football quickly. He wants to arrive where the ball is and be in a bad mood when he gets there.

That's why a guy like Dick Butkus, Chicago Bears middle linebacker from 1965 to 1973, picked up the nicknames "The Enforcer," "The Animal," and the "Robot of Destruction." He was a Hall of Fame player who is described on *chicagobears.com* as follows: "He had drive, meanness, a consuming desire to pursue, tackle, butt and manhandle-anything he could do to thwart the enemy on every play. Still he was a clean football player, fantastically devoted to his career, a man who by his own admission played every game as though it were his last one."

Every linebacker is a warrior at heart or as the title of John Eldredge's remarkable book would call it, each one is *Wild at Heart*[17]. Every man was once a boy with big dreams. Maybe his dream wasn't to excel in sports, but for many that has been the ultimate dream. Only a few grow up to be a Butkus, Singletary, or Nitschke. For the rest those dreams change or go unfulfilled.

Still, in the heart of each man there is an underlying fear. Men need to be strong and courageous. But, there is only one way to achieve that. It comes by trusting God. After all those years of wandering in the wilderness, the children of Israel were finally poised to enter the Promised Land. Their leader was Joshua. What an awesome responsibility he had—to finally conquer the land of their dreams. Joshua needed a linebacker's mentality.

But, as Eldredge says, "Joshua knew what it was to be afraid." So, God had to remind him: *Be strong and courageous, because you will lead these people to inherit the land I swore to their forefathers to give them. Be strong and very courageous...Have I not commanded you Be strong and courageous. Do not be terrified; do not be discouraged, for the Lord your God will be with you wherever you go. Joshua 1:6-7,9.*[18]

Joshua had good reason to feel overwhelmed by his task. Over a million people had wandered through the wilderness during those 40 years before God finally led them to Canaan. Joshua and Caleb were the only two who had left Egypt and were going to enter the Promised Land. As Joshua watched others fall by the wayside or die, the size of his responsibility grew to mammoth proportions.

That's why God kept reminding him be strong and courageous. Don't be afraid. Don't get discouraged. Joshua could have said, "Oh sure, that's easy for you to say, God. But I've got a whole fearful nation waiting for me to lead them into a land where we don't know what awaits us." But God added, "the Lord your God will be with you wherever you go."

There's an old saying, "if the Lord leads you to it, he will lead you through it." God had lead Joshua to the Promised Land. Now, he was going to lead him through the Promised Land. He reiterated that because he didn't want Joshua to lose sight of that fact. We often lose sight of that because we are trying to look ahead into an unknown future, instead of trusting God to lead us into and through it.

Mike Singletary was led to the brink of disaster. While in junior high his parents divorced and his brother, Brady, was killed at the age of 22 in an auto accident caused by a drunk driver. Those events made him realize how short life is and made him determined to do his best.

The quiet, thoughtful Singletary became known as "Samurai Mike" because of the ferociousness of the hits he put on ball carriers. At Baylor, he actually cracked 16 helmets and was once credited with 33 tackles in a game against Arkansas.

With the Chicago Bears Singletary become known as a big game player because of his preparation. Normally on the quiet side he became so fired up before the 1985 NFC championship game against the Rams that he gave a little impromptu "Knute Rockne talk" that had the Bears players so excited they were throwing tables and chairs. Then Singletary went out and hit all-pro RB Eric Dickerson so hard that, according to fellow linebacker Wilbur Marshall, "I don't think he (Dickerson) knew where he was."[19]

Despite disaster in his life, Mike Singletary was able to approach each opponent with boldness because of his thorough preparation and determination to succeed. When we prepare to meet each day through Bible Study and communication with God through prayer, we also can follow God's instructions to Joshua to be strong and courageous.

# Prayer for Guidance

Lord, we are often too aware of our weaknesses and feel inadequate when it comes to dealing with our problems. Give us the linebacker mentality to start each day by fully preparing ourselves through Bible Study and prayer. We know when we use the tools and talents you have given us in the way you direct us, we can then be strong and courageous.

Amen.

## Chapter Eight

# THE RUNNING BACKS

> *Do you not know that in a race all the runners run,*
> *But only one gets the prize?*
> *Run in such a way as to get the prize.*
>
> I Corinthians 9:24

It doesn't matter how fast a runner you are, how quickly you can cut, if you have the strength to run over tacklers, or the ability to spin in a circle and keep your feet, there is one thing that can negate all of that—a fumble. The unpardonable sin for a runner is to fumble the football.

Legendary Georgia Tech football coach John Heisman used to start out the season by holding up a football and telling his running backs, "Gentlemen, it is better to have died as a small boy than to fumble this football."[20]

Running backs come in all shapes and sizes. Red Grange, who became one of the all-time greats, wasn't all that big. He was only five-foot-eleven, 175 pounds. He said, "If you have the football and 11 guys are after you, if you're smart you'll run."

And run he did—with speed and elusiveness. In a 1924 game against a Michigan team that had only allowed four TDs in two full seasons, Grange scored four touchdowns and gained 262 yards in 12 minutes. After that effort the immortal Grantland Rice described the Illinois running back this way:

> *A streak of fire, a breath of flame*
> *eluding all who reach and clutch*
> *a gray ghost thrown into the game*
> *that rival hands may never touch,*
> *a rubber bounding, blasting soul*
> *whose destination is the goal.*

Forever after, the Illinois RB would be known as the "Galloping Ghost." Damon Runyan said Grange was four men rolled into one. Runyan named them: Jack Dempsey, Babe Ruth, Al Jolson, Paavo Nurmi and he threw in Man o' War for good measure.[22]

Needless to say, the Fightin' Illini and eventually the Chicago Bears got all the help they needed to succeed from a ghost…the Galloping Ghost—Red Grange. As believers in Christ we receive help from a ghost—the Holy Ghost, as the Holy Spirit is sometimes referred to. In **John 14:15–18 Jesus says, *If you love me, obey my commandments. And I will ask the Father, and He will give you another Counselor, who will never leave you. He is the Holy Spirit who leads into all truth. The world at large, cannot receive him, because it isn't looking for him, and doesn't recognize him. But, you do because he lives with you now and later will be in you.***

Thus, when Jesus returned to heaven after his resurrection he realized we were going to need help down here. So He sent a

Counselor to in-dwell us, a counselor who was a member of the Trinity—the Holy Spirit. All believers received the Holy Spirit who would guide them.

Still, there is no promise that the road will be an easy one. Jesus discovered that himself; *Then Jesus, full of the Holy Spirit, left the Jordan River. He was led by the Spirit to go out into the wilderness, where the Devil tempted him for forty days.* So, it is not all going to be peaches and cream because we have the Holy Spirit. But the Life Application Bible, New Living Translation advises, "When facing trials, first make sure you haven't brought them on yourself through sin or unwise choices. If you find no sin to confess or unwise behavior to change, then ask God to strengthen you for your test. Finally, be careful to follow faithfully wherever the Holy Spirit leads."[23]

The Army team found a way to defeat enemy defenses with the running game in the 1940's by following the lead of Mr. Inside and Mr. Outside. For the Knights of the Hudson, Mr. Inside was powerful running fullback Doc Blanchard, a South Carolinian who trampled defenders. Mr. Outside was the lithe halfback, Glenn Davis, a California born speedster who loved to run around defenses. They led Army to a 27–0–1 record and two national titles between 1944 and 1946.

After a game in 1944 Notre Dame coach Ed McKeever said, "I've just seen Superman in the flesh. He wears number 35 and goes by the name of Blanchard." In 1945, playing before President Harry Truman and 102,000 fans, Blanchard scored three touchdowns, leading Army to a 32–13 thrashing of Navy. On one TD he was described as running through a tackler "as if he were a paper bag." Blanchard became the first junior to win the Heisman Trophy, no mean accomplishment since he split some votes with teammate Davis, who finished as runner up.

Not to be dismayed, Glenn Davis won the Heisman Trophy in 1946 and finished his career with 2,957 yards, 59 touchdowns (still an Army record), and varsity letters in football, baseball, basketball, and track. Later he dated Elizabeth Taylor and was called by the New York Times, "the best halfback football has produced in modern times." The stock of running backs in college football was never higher than the Davis-Blanchard years at Army, when Mr. Inside and Mr. Outside ruled the gridiron game.

These two runners formed a close bond as they fought together for victories on the gridiron, but maybe no two backs ever had a closer friendship than Gayle Sayres and Brian Piccolo. An unlikely pair to develop a friendship...Sayres the speedy running back from Kansas and Piccolo the Florida-born fullback who matriculated at Wake Forest. When they became teammates on the Chicago Bears a friendship was forged; but as Sayres became a superstar, Piccolo became very sick—with cancer. Sayres stayed by Piccolo until the end, encouraging him and in turn being bolstered by Piccolo's courage as he fought the dreaded disease. The movie "Brian's Song" was based on this story of the undying friendship between two running backs, one black and one white, who became friends closer than brothers. Much of the screenplay was adapted from Sayres' book called *I am Third* in which he said that he was third in his life behind God, family, and friends like Brian Piccolo.

Brian Piccolo and Gayle Sayres were two running backs who were friends to the end. The Holy Spirit is a friend we have who will be with us always; one who will help us run the race in such a way as to get the prize.

## Prayer for Guidance

Lord, sometimes running is what we do best. We run here and there at breakneck speed, but gain no advantage, only frustration in our lives. Help us to daily seek the Holy Spirit's help that we might run the course laid out before us, keeping our eye on the ultimate prize you have for us.

Amen!

## Chapter Nine

# THE DEFENSIVE LINE

*Put on all of God's armor so you will be able to stand firm against all strategies and tricks of the Devil.*

**Ephesians 6:11**

There was a lone cowpoke who went riding out on a dark, windy day. Resting on a ridge, a bolt of fear went through him when he saw a bunch of gaunt, solemn-faced riders chasing a herd of red-eyed cows whose brands were still on fire. Read carefully what transpired next:

*The cowpokes rode on past him and he heard one call his name,*
*If you want to save your soul from hell a-riding on the range,*
*Then cowboy change your ways today, or with us you will ride,*
*A-trying to catch the devil's herd across these endless skies.*

*Yippee-yi-yo, yippee-yi, the ghost riders in the sky.* [24]

A word of warning from the popular song, *Ghost Riders in the Sky,* by Vaughn Monroe that rose to number one on the charts in 1949 and was subsequently recorded by Bing Crosby, Peggy Lee, Frankie Lane, and others. The song tells us that to avoid a devil-led defeat we must change our ways and arm ourselves for warfare by putting on God's armor. Every day it is a battle in the trenches and it takes all the protection we can get to keep from being out-tricked, out-smarted, or out-muscled by those negative forces.

In the football trenches the protector of a team's territory is the defense, led by the defensive line. The DL is the first line of defense. They line up inches from the battle line—the line of scrimmage. These men must stand firm against every offensive strategy to ensure victory. They must become experts at reacting quickly, fighting off blocks, and getting to the ball.

In the 1960's the Los Angeles Rams' Fearsome Foursome glamorized the work of the defensive line. This group, consisting of Lamar Lundy, Rosey Grier, Merlin Olson, and Deacon Jones, was constantly in the opposing backfield. "They gang tackled…pursued plays…sacked quarterbacks. They had the ability to bull rush any offensive line. They would stunt and cause confusion to opposing offenses. They even would rotate their positions during the game."[25]

A typical NFL defensive line consists of two ends and two tackles. Their job is to gum up the works—stop the run, rush the passer. In college there will often be a fifth lineman called a nose-guard who plays in the middle of the defensive line. This player is usually the most dominating player on the defense, often requiring double-team blocking to negate his strength and quickness.

According to Bobby Bowden, the road to becoming a top-ranked program during his early days at Florida State was due, in large part, to a nose-guard. "It's hard to say one man can make or break your program, but look what Tony Dorsett did for Pitt. We feel the same way about Ron (Simmons)," said Bowden.

Ron Simmons was the ultimate strongman. When he was only a freshman, Simmons bench-pressed 435 pounds. But he also possessed great speed and used it to rack up an unbelievable 19 tackles in a single game in his first season. Veteran Sports-writer Tom McEwen (Tampa Tribune) had the classic description of Simmons, one that still fronts his biography: "Simmons wasn't born. He was chiseled out of brown Georgia granite, had the wings of mercury attached to his ankles and had life breathed into him by whatever saint is assigned to Bobby Bowden.

"Simmons was fully equipped to defend Seminole Territory against all tactics. He had the strength to fight off blockers and stop even the strongest of running backs, or the speed to chase a runner down from behind or put pressure on the passer. In Ephesians the Apostle Paul talks about the various stratagems that the devil employs—discouragement, frustration, confusion, moral failure, and doctrinal error. He knows our weakest point and aims for it. If he cannot disable us by one method, he will try for another." [26]

So, the way to protect our lives is to be fully armed with God's defenses. Paul says to put on the belt of truth, the breastplate of righteousness, the shoes to spread the gospel of peace, the helmet of salvation, and the sword of the Spirit (the word of God).

Bill Glass was an All-American defensive lineman at Baylor where he helped lead the Bears to four bowl games. Later he became an All-Pro with the Cleveland Browns, winning three division championships. Glass armed himself so fully with God's armor that he never missed a game or even a practice during 10 years of playing football in school (high school and college) or 12 years in the Pros until the last four games of his career. It is an amazing feat of stamina and determination.

Glass committed his career to the Lord and gave his testimony freely. He appeared on television several times with Billy Graham during his evangelistic crusade. He attended Southwestern Theological Seminary in the off-season and after his football career ended, Graham urged him to become a full-time evangelist. He started Champions for Life as a part of the Bill Glass Evangelistic Association in 1969 and it is still going strong. He has led thousands to Christ, especially in his Prison Ministry.

Bill Glass was a winner as a defensive lineman. He has written 11 books, most of which deal with winning. Some of his book titles include: *Expect to Win, Plan to Win* and *How to Win When the Roof Caves in.* Glass knows that to win, you must have the proper plan and it includes being armed with wisdom from God. On his crusades he talks about "the four spiritual laws that govern your relationship with God." These laws point out that; (1) God loves us and has a plan for us; (2) Man is sinful and is separated from God; (3) Jesus Christ is God's provision for man's sin; (4) When we receive Jesus as Savior then we can know and experience God's love and plan for us. Glass says our "self-directed life" then becomes a "Christ-directed life."[27]

Goal-line stands are often the difference between winning and losing a game and the defensive line usually leads the way. When the offense gets in the red zone, the defenders must step up, take their game to another level, and play stellar defense. It starts with the surge of the defensive line. The DL must win the battle in the trenches or the defense will be pushed back into the end zone. It takes God's armor for the enemy's advance to be stopped and victory to be achieved.

## Prayer for Guidance

There are so many strategies that must be defended against in our efforts to lead a Christ-centered life, Lord, that we often feel like we are waging a losing battle. A little of our territory keeps disappearing, piece-by-piece, over time. In our lives and in our country we see times changing, morals slipping, and easy acceptance of things that were once forbidden. These practices have insinuated themselves into our lives and as our children grow up with them, these sins have become too easily accepted. Lord, equip us with the armor we need to dig in, defend our territory for Christ, and reverse these trends.

Amen.

## Chapter Ten
# THE OFFENSIVE LINE

> *He trains my hands for battle;*
> *my arms can bend a bow of bronze.*
>
> Psalm 18:34

**M**ammoth Men, weighing 300 pounds or more. Most stand six-foot-two or taller. Heavily muscled. Quick feet. Physically talented, key members of the offensive operation. If their blocks are not made, everything breaks down. So why do they labor in anonymity, their work often unacknowledged and un-appreciated?

Let Joe Montana, Emmit Smith, or Jerry Rice walk into a store and they are besieged with autograph requests. If John Hannah, Art Shell, or Forrest Gregg stroll the aisles of the local Wal-Mart, it's likely that not many people, except for the most hard-core of fans, would recognize them. The guards, tackles, and centers on a football team just aren't in the limelight that much.

Rarely do offensive linemen score a touchdown. Most often they don't even touch the ball and only when a fumble or interception occurs would they be called on to make a tackle. In the gridiron game, whoever has the football attracts the most attention. It's usually a fluke when an offensive lineman touches the ball except to snap or recover it.

However, they are usually the biggest guys on the team. John Hannah, whose picture once graced the cover of a *Sports Illustrated* magazine that called him the "greatest offensive lineman of all time," weighed 35 pounds when he was only a year old. Hannah grew up to weigh a paltry 265 pounds, but because of his strong legs and powerful arms he was able to block even the most dominating defensive players. Hannah was a first round pick in 1973 by the Patriots out of the University of Alabama where he was a two-time All-American. He played 13 seasons in the NFL and was inducted into the Hall of Fame indicating he was one of the best and most aggressive blockers ever.[28]

Blocking is what the offensive line is all about. Sacrificing the body to keep anyone from getting to the quarterback, or knocking a defender out of the way to make a hole for a running back to go through.

Sometimes a lineman will be thrust into the spotlight and receive the publicity he has earned. These rare occasions are ones to be celebrated by all linemen. This was the case for Jerry Kramer, who happened to have his number called in a never-to-be-forgotten game played under the most adverse weather conditions in the history of the National Football League.

On New Year's Eve, 1967, the Packers and Cowboys played for the NFL championship in Green Bay on Lambeau Field. It was the game that would forever associate the term "frozen tundra" with Lambeau. It was played in temperatures of 13 degrees below zero.

With 16 seconds remaining and everyone battling frostbite and fatigue, the Packers were on the Cowboys two-foot line—just 24 frozen inches from the end zone—trailing 17–14. A field goal would tie the game and subject everyone to an excruciating overtime in the bitter cold. The footing had become treacherous, the conditions almost unbearable. What would the great coach Vince Lombardi call? The field goal unit was warming up when Lombardi sent in the play. No field goal! Disdaining the tie, he instructed quarterback Bart Starr to try a quarterback sneak behind guard Jerry Kramer. Struggling to dig into the frozen ground, Kramer reached back for something extra. He threw what is still referred to as the "block of the century," knocking Cowboy DL Jethro Pugh back as Starr dove into the end zone with the winning score.[29] Kramer would later chronicle the play and the game in the book *Instant Replay* that became one of the all-time best-selling sports books.

It is obvious that offensive linemen need great strength to do their job and at every position they must practice their craft to improve. Our strength is in the Lord, but we must practice to get stronger to perform His plan better. As a football team's opponents are practicing to win, so are the evil forces we must battle against. New strategies and new roadblocks to success are thrown at us constantly.

**Psalm 18:32** says *God arms me with strength and makes my way safe.* But the key here is to be fighting within God's will, within His plan, so he can strengthen our efforts and enable us to fight the battle with maximum strength.

The New Living Translation says, "God promises to give us strength to meet challenges, but he doesn't promise to eliminate them. If He gave us no rough roads to walk, no mountains to climb, and no battles to fight we would not grow. He does not leave us alone with our challenges, however, instead He stands beside us, teaches us, and strengthens us to face them."[30]

We must heed His instructions. If Jerry Kramer had said to Coach Lombardi, "Coach, this footing is too unstable. I don't think I can get enough traction to block out a big guy like Jethro Pugh," then the Packers might have lost the championship game. But he had confidence in Coach Lombardi's play selection and his wisdom. Lombardi's greatness lay in his ability to sell his ideas to the players so they would give every ounce of energy to the cause. In addition, he did it in a very intimidating way; one in which you wouldn't even dare to question.

Forrest Gregg, the six-foot-four, 250 tackle in that Ice Bowl Game said, "When Lombardi says to sit down, you don't look for a chair." The troops believed in him. In return, Lombardi justified his demands by saying, "Once a man has made a commitment to a way of life, he puts the greatest strength in the world behind him. It's something we call heart power…"

Dave Van Halanger, the respected Christian strength coach of the Georgia Bulldogs, is a former offensive lineman. The main thing he tries to develop in his players is what he calls "explosive power." By stretching and strengthening their muscles, his players become capable of exploding off the ball when it is snapped. When he counsels with players he also inquires if their heart is right with the Lord.

By strengthening our commitment to playing life's game God's way, we will develop the heart power and explosiveness that will knock down any roadblock and bring victory in our lives.

## Prayer for Guidance

Lord, as we look at the role of the successful offensive linemen, we see that their job is to subvert ego and headline-seeking to the good of the team. May we learn from this. It is not about us, but about you and your glory and helping others to make the commitment that leads to heart power that cannot be defeated.

Amen!

## Chapter Eleven

# THE SECONDARY

> *(Jacob) made a richly ornamented robe for him (Joseph). When his brothers saw that their father loved him more than any of them, they hated him and could not speak a kind word to him.*
>
> Genesis 37: 3b, 4

Colorful! Confident! Cocky! These are all terms that could apply to the football players who line up in the secondary—the defensive backs. It takes a unique talent to master running full speed backwards without falling, then sprinting along side a speedy receiver, stopping, cutting, and changing directions while keeping your balance and knowing where you are on the field at all times. Not only that, the defensive back must keep his eyes on the ball and the receiver at the same time. Complicating matters is the fact that the receiver knows where he is going, but the DB doesn't. No wonder it requires supreme self-confidence to play in the secondary.

The secondary consists of cornerbacks and safeties. The cornerbacks usually line up on the corners (go figure) and are matched up against the opponents best pass catchers—the wide-receivers. The safeties are usually fast, powerful players, who line up deepest in the secondary and must deal with the tight ends as receivers, provide support in stopping the run, and help in defending wide receivers and running backs on pass plays.

Defensive backs must also know the (pass) coverage that has been called which basically falls into two categories; man-to-man or zone coverage. It is obvious that the DB has a lot on his mind because the slightest mistake means a touchdown for the opponent. So, the last thing a DB must do is show any sign that he is intimidated by another player.

Deion Sanders, considered by some the greatest cornerback to play the game, was asked if he was going to tone down his cockiness after he had become a Christian. Deion said that the way he saw it, the Lord wanted to change his heart, not his personality. So, Neon Deion did his thing as controversy continued to surround his playing style through a career that included successful stops at Florida State University, Dallas, San Francisco, and Washington (also the Reds, Yankees, and Braves in baseball) before retiring to the Broadcast booth.

In a *Sporting News* article Paul Attner wrote, "If Deion had never been Prime Time, never had talked the talk, never had been a walking Tiffany's display case, never had strutted and danced and rapped and gloated, never had worn one of those lavender suits, there wouldn't be the controversy that always surrounds his swagger." But, Deion thrived on it. His cockiness led to his success.

In the Bible there was another cocky guy and sharp dresser we can all learn from. His name was Joseph. It was bad enough that when he was a teenager his father, Jacob, made him this fancy coat that showed favoritism over his brothers. But it was the swagger that accompanied it that caused the controversy.

In a day when everyone wore a robe or a cloak, most were knee length, short sleeved, and plain. But the one Jacob made for Joseph was apparently very colorful, long-sleeved, and ankle length.[31] It was bad enough that Joseph had this fancy coat and his brothers had ordinary ones, but he called them together and told them about a dream he had.

*"Listen to this dream," he announced. "We were out in the field tying up bundles of grain. My bundle stood, and then your bundles all gathered around and bowed low before it."* **Genesis 37: 6–7.** You can imagine how happy his brothers were with that little story. They taunted him saying, "So, you're going to be king over us, huh?"

Of course they determined to show the little braggart a thing or two. They grabbed Joseph, threw him in a well, and left him there until a caravan of Egyptian traders came along. Then his brothers sold Joseph to be a slave.

What evolved from all of this was one of the greatest examples in the Bible of how God can use events that man intends for evil and bring good out of them. Joseph was confident because he was very bright and he trusted God. So as he rose through the ranks in a foreign land, God blessed him and he became Governor. When a great famine hit the land and Joseph's brothers had to come to Egypt to find food, they indeed did end up bowing down before him as an official of the King to obtain food for survival.

Often we don't understand why things are happening the way they are in our lives. We seem to be thrust out on an island like a cornerback. We have to run as fast as we can and be ready to switch directions without even knowing where we are going. Our confidence comes not only from the ability God has given us to deal with these situations, but from knowing that He is in control. Even if it seems like it is a bad thing that is happening to us, God can use it for good.

The Detroit Lions had a great cornerback named Dick "Night Train" Lane. He got his nickname from a his favorite song by the same name in the 50's. Some people thought he got the name from receivers he smashed who felt like they had been hit by a train. Teammate Joe Schmidt, a fellow Hall of Famer, said, "Train had great size and speed. I have never seen anyone with the type of closing speed on a receiver that he had. Train took pride in getting to the receiver and making the tackle. He also was a true team player. Whatever he did, he did it for the team."

Talk about supreme confidence, Lane—with scrapbook in hand—talked his way past the secretaries in the Los Angles Rams Hollywood office and into the office of Coach Joe Stydahar, who had once seen him play in the army. Lane then talked his way into a spot on the team and a $4,500 bonus. He said, "I was a small, very wiry kid so therefore nobody gave me a ghost of a chance of making it. But, I had a big heart."[32]

Like Neon Deion and Night Train, no matter how much swagger they showed on the outside, the inside was strong. If the heart is set on the ways of the Lord and how the talents may be used to honor him, the swagger is justified. It's more than talking the talk, it's about showing them you can walk the walk and succeed despite the obstacles that must be overcome.

## Prayer for Guidance

Lord, we sometimes feel that we are called on to do so many things with very little margin for error. We try to remain confident, to feel the inner arrogance that comes from knowing we will succeed. But, that arrogance, swagger, and confidence can only manifest itself if you endow us with it and enable us to use it. No matter what our personality traits are, we commit them to you and ask that you take and use them for good in all the circumstances we find ourselves in.

Amen!

# Chapter 12

# THE KICKERS

> *You will keep in perfect peace Him whose mind is steadfast, because He trusts in you.*
>
> Isaiah 26:3

**M**ental toughness! It's what every coach looks for in his players. A mindset that says, "I can do it," is important at every position. It is an absolute necessity for the place kicker. Many times the outcome of the game rests in the hands, uh, foot of the player who is usually the smallest guy on the field. In fact, the kicker can sometimes be outweighed by as much as 200 pounds by a teammate or opposing player. So, it is imperative that this little guy thinks big!

Of course not all kickers are small. Lou Groza was big… lineman big. At six-foot-three, 240 pounds he played offensive tackle for the Cleveland Browns for 14 seasons. Groza was named to nine Pro Bowl teams and in 1954 was the NFL Player of the Year.

But the main thing Groza will always be known for is kicking field goals. He put field goals on the National Football League map. "Before Lou Groza field goals weren't much of a weapon in the NFL," said teammate and fellow Hall of Fame member Dante Lavelli. "Nobody kicked like Lou before Lou."[33]

Groza's three-pointers, achieved with his own straight-on, kick-off-the-toe style, became such a weapon that he was given the nickname "The Toe." Groza never had time to worry about whether a drive would stall and leave him with a long kick. He was too busy blocking defensive players to notice. But when the offense was stopped, he was ready.

It takes a focused mind to kick a field goal. The holder sets up seven to eight yards behind the center and kneels down on one knee. The kicker marks off the steps he will take. When the ball is snapped, the kicker has no more than 1.3 seconds to get the kick off and up above the on-rushing linemen and through the goal posts. The kickers' thoughts must be fixed on one thing—making the kick. If he thinks about how important the kick is and what it means to the team, or the on-rushing kick-blockers, or worries that the ball won't be snapped properly, or the holder might not catch it cleanly or will fail to spin the laces around so he doesn't kick them, his mind will be diverted from the proper technique to make the kick. There are so many things that he must trust will happen as he focuses only on the kick itself.

**Isaiah 26:3** would be a good verse for a kicker to tape inside his helmet. It simply says to trust God and keep your thoughts fixed on him and you'll have peace of mind. With a calm mind you can accomplish great things.

The New Living Translation commentary on that verse makes some good points. "We can never avoid strife in the world around us, but when we fix our thoughts on God, we can know perfect peace even in turmoil. As we focus our mind on God and his Word, we become steady, and stable. Supported by God's unchanging love and mighty power we are not shaken by the surrounding chaos."

Staying focused on God prepares us for the twists and turns our lives take. It seems the path to success is never straight. John Riley was an All-SEC place kicker for Auburn. After college he signed a contract to kick for the Oakland Raiders. John was a Christian, but he says he knows now he wasn't focused on God's plan back then. "I figured I would go out and kick field goals and make a bunch of money during football season, and in the off season I'd spend my time hunting and fishing. Then, maybe once a month, I'd give a talk at some church. What a great deal for God," Riley said with a smile.[34]

But God had other plans for John Riley. A freak injury tore up his knee and he had a lot of time to focus his thoughts on God while sitting on his front porch in Abbeville, Alabama as his knee mended. He never kicked another football, but he did become one of the most dynamic and entertaining lay speakers in America. He has spoken to countless churches and businesses in the USA and overseas. His appeal to people of all ages and from all walks of life has been greatly used by the Lord.

At Oakland, Riley would have been competing for the kicking job with a guy by the name of George Blanda. God had a pretty amazing plan in mind for Blanda as well. George ended up becoming a legend for the over-forty football fans because he was a field-goal kicker and quarterback until shortly before his forty-ninth birthday.

Blanda had a fairly undistinguished career as a quarterback with the Chicago Bears and retired in 1959 because they wanted to use him only as a kicker. Then, in 1960 he joined the Houston Oilers in the new American Football League. In 1967, he was traded to the Raiders.

In one amazing five-week stretch in1970, at the age of forty-three, Blanda won five straight games for the Raiders. He filled in for injured QB Daryle LaMonica and threw three touchdown passes to beat Pittsburgh. The next week he kicked a 48-yard field goal with three seconds left to tie Kansas City. He came in the following week trailing by a touchdown and threw a 14-yard TD pass to tie the game. Then Blanda won it with a 52-yard field goal. On November 15th he entered the game with four minutes left, losing 19–17 and marched the Raiders 80 yards hitting Fred Biletnikoff with a 20-yard TD pass to win the game. On November 22nd, Blanda kicked a 16-yard field goal with four seconds remaining to give Oakland a 20–17 win over San Diego. [36]

When George Blanda finally retired, he had played pro football for 26 years, kicked 943 extra points, 225 field goals, and scored 2,002 points. Being a field goal kicker had prolonged and eventually became the focus of his career.

The key is to block out those distractions and use your talents in the way God is directing you at the moment. By fixing your thoughts on God, you'll receive the peace of mind to help you get the biggest kick out of life.

# Prayer for Guidance

Lord, as we picture in our minds the field goal kicker, we see him focused on the spot where the ball will be placed. He avoids the distractions that would keep him from making the kick and trusts his teammates to protect him. May we learn from this example to fix our attention on you. As our thoughts turn to your plan to trust you to protect us, so our minds will be stabilized for the work ahead of us.

Amen.

## Chapter Thirteen
# SPECIAL TEAMS

*All a man's ways seem right to him,*
*but the Lord weighs the heart.*

### Proverbs 21:2

" **Y** ou gotta have heart
All you really need is heart
When the odds are sayin'
You'll never win
That's when a grin
should start...

You gotta have heart
Miles 'n' miles 'n' miles of heart!
Oh, it's fine to be a genius of course,
But keep that old horse before the cart,
First you gotta have heart!"[37]

A rag-tag bunch of ballplayers sang that song in the musical *Damn Yankees*. Because they had "heart," they were transformed from losers to winners.

Playing on special teams is not for the faint of heart. Football coaches look for special teams players who have "miles 'n' miles 'n' miles of heart." Only players with a big heart need apply.

The guys who do the kicking, return the kicks, block during the kicks, and cover the kicks are referred to as special teams players. You don't necessarily have to be fast to play on special teams. What you have to be is, uh, crazy! You have to play more with your heart than your head. When you run down the field full-speed and collide with another big body going full speed, something has got to give. When you run full tilt and stretch out in front of a guy punting the football, it ain't gonna feel too good when you get kicked. But these special teams players must play with reckless abandon because games can be won or lost on special teams.

George Allen, the legendary NFL coach and reknowned work-a-holic, worked relentlessly on special teams play when he coached the Washington Redskins. Allen, concerning why he worked on special teams so much, once said, "Every day you waste is one you can't make up."[38] He told his coaches that one-third of a team's season is wrapped up in special teams. He even wrote a book called *George Allen's Guide to Special Teams.*[39] In it he discussed every possible aspect of special teams play. He was a stickler for detail and felt that every player had to be in just the right position on the field on every play to have a chance to win the game.

Special teams play is so crucial it is imperative that you have players committed to winning—players with heart—on those teams. In his book *Wild at Heart,* John Eldredge says that every man must have a battle to fight. Each man must have a mission that transcends even home and family that he is devoted to even unto death. That is why God created you and he has given you a warrior's heart to win the battle.[40]

In the movie *Braveheart,* William Wallace, played by Mel Gibson, was a poet. He became a warrior and the liberator of his people in the early 1300's. The Scots were floundering around with no leader and were about to lose heart as the evil English King Edward the Longshanks ran roughshod over Scotland. But along came Wallace, a man with a braveheart, who took a band of warriors and built them into a force that would overcome the English Army and restore his country's freedom.[41]

You've heard the saying "his heart is in the right place." Well, everybody's heart is in the same place. It is what your heart is tuned to that makes a difference. How wonderful would it be to be described as "a man after God's heart." That was the description given to King David in the Bible. Like David, we have all found favor with God in some things we do. Also like David we have all gone astray.

The key is the course your heart is set on. **Proverbs 23:7 *For as a man thinketh in his heart so is he. (KJV)*** In a later book, *Waking the Dead,* John Eldredge says, "Our deepest thoughts are held in our hearts." You believe with your heart.[42] You are motivated to act by your heart.

Special teams players, the guys with heart, are also some of the most overlooked players when it comes to receiving credit from the media and fans for their roles in the game. For proof of this you have only to look at the Pro Football Hall of Fame and see how few special teams players are in there.

Brian Mitchell has made a pretty good living as a special teams player. In 13 seasons with the Redskins and Eagles he has returned kickoffs for 12,897 yards and punts for 4,845 yards and 13 touchdowns. He makes a good point for including more special teams players in the Hall of Fame. "It's the Pro Football Hall of Fame," he told Philadelphia Inquirer reporter Mike Bruton. "It's not the Pro Football Offensive and Defensive Hall of Fame. It doesn't make sense. If you're going to keep stats for kickers, returners, and punters and all that type of stuff, why not allow them in."[43]

Football is a game of field position. Usually the team that is continually starting drives from the best field position wins the game. Through the efforts of the special teams a team gains good field position or gets stuck with a bad starting point.

George Allen won over 70% of the games he coached. It is no coincidence that he was the first head coach to hire a special teams coach. That was way back in 1948 when he was the coach at Morningside College. It's hard to say how many victories he achieved in his career as a result of attention paid to special teams play, but it is safe to say his special teams won a whole lot more games for him than they lost.

A job one special teams player has is holding the football for kicks. A writer once asked John Brodie, the 49ers superstar quarterback, why he had to perform the lowly job of holding the football for kicks. Brodie replied, "Somebody's got to hold the ball up or it will fall over." Whatever it takes to get the job done—that's what a special teams player must do.

In the final analysis of just how important special teams are, Brian Mitchell said it best. "You can't start the game without them." That's right! So next time a football game gets underway, observe

74

closely those 22 players on the field. They'll be the ones with "miles 'n' miles 'n' miles of heart."

## Prayer for Guidance

Lord, just being on your team makes us a part of a special team. Help us to set our hearts on a course that will win the battles, big or small, in your name. May our thoughts be governed by a discerning heart, one that is strong and determined to do your will and win in the game of life.

Amen

## Chapter Fourteen

# THE GOAL LINE

> *When Pharaoh finally let the people go, God did not
> lead them on the road that runs through Philistine territory
> even though that was the shortest way from Egypt to
> the Promised Land...So God led them along the Wilderness
> toward the Red Sea.*
>
> Exodus 13:17-18

C rossing the goal line. Boiled down to it's simplest explanation, that's what the game of football is all about. It's kind of like the description of how to succeed in baseball that simply says simply, "See ball, hit ball." It isn't that easy. There are a lot of factors that come into play when you're trying to put a bat on a high speed, spinning, dipping baseball. Likewise, getting the ball across that goal line isn't easy when there are eleven guys on the other side whose mission is to see to it that you don't.

You can cross the goal line by land or air. Sometimes you have to take the long route, if you start deep in your territory. But the time required to negotiate that route can be shortened considerably by completing a bomb. Other times it just takes patience to cover the ground to the goal line with a time-consuming drive of 10 or 12, sometimes as many as 18, plays to get there. But getting your team in position to score is the key.

Often in life, positioning is the real way to succeed. By studying, practicing, and praying you get yourself in position to be successful when God puts the opportunity to cross the goal line in front of you. My wife, the lovely Susette, spent many years working in businesses connected with the interior design industry. She studied design in college. She tried her own business a couple of times. Then she worked for commercial furnishing stores and free-lanced in residential interior design.

Then, one day when she had all that experience and was in position to be successful, the Lord directed her to open her own interior design business. Calling on all that experience and working within God's timing, Affinity Design Group enjoyed immediate success. She had gotten herself in position to succeed.

Soon after she opened her business she bought a small aquarium for her office with three fish swimming in it. Two were goldfish and one was a gold and black spotted fish. She named them Affinity, Infinity, and Divinity. These fish learned quickly when someone approached the aquarium and turned on the light that they would get fed. They immediately would swim to the top of the aquarium and get in position for the food that would inevitably come floating downward.

Sometimes the position God requires us to be in before we succeed can be confusingly circuitous. An example was described in **Exodus 13:17-18.** When they had escaped Egypt, God did not take the Israelites on the direct route to the Promised Land. As always, God had his reasons.

The New Living Translation says "God doesn't always work in the way that seems best to us. Instead of guiding the Israelites along the direct route from Egypt to the Promised Land, he took them by a longer route to avoid fighting with the Philistines. If God does not lead you along the shortest path to your goal, don't complain or resist. Follow Him willingly and trust Him to lead you safely around unseen obstacles. He can see the end of your journey from the beginning and he knows the safest and best route."

Sometimes a football team will get down to the goal line, in position to score, and will not be able to get it into the end zone. When they are thinking run, the defense is anticipating run and they get stopped. If they think pass with the defense playing pass defense, they fail. So, just being in position does not guarantee success.

It is what you do with the talents you are given once you are in position that gives you the winning edge. Often it requires help. One powerful runner going into several big, strong, poorly-blocked linemen will not score despite the running back's talents. A strong armed quarterback cannot throw the football through a defensive back who cuts in front of the receiver. The right decision made from the right position is the most important thing.

On September 13, 1988, the Florida State Seminoles were definitely not in position to cross the goal line. With the ball deep in their territory, FSU was facing a fourth down late in the game. The score was tied at 21–21. Clemson would surely get the ball in good field position.

Coach Bobby Bowden could see the whole season passing in front of his very eyes and this was only the second game. The

Seminoles had been ranked number one to begin the season, but had been trounced 31–0 in the season opener at Miami. A loss here and they could kiss not only their hopes for a shot at the national championship goodbye, but any possibility of a top five finish.

How could they possibly get in field position to score? Anything but a punt would probably not work. But if they gave the ball up to Clemson, they would surely not get it back and the Tigers, behind a loud home crowd at Death Valley, could put the game away with a field goal.

At that point Bowden decided there was only one route to take. It was not the shortest or most likely one. It was a gamble, but, he took it. He called for the puntrooskie—a trick play his Seminoles had not used before. After the ball was snapped the punter leaped high in the air, then turned and ran toward the FSU goal in an apparent attempt to chase down an errant snap.

But, unspotted by almost everyone in the stands and just about everyone on the Clemson team, the ball had really been snapped short to LeRoy Butler, who had set up in a blocking position. Butler took off around left end and was not stopped until he was knocked out of bounds at the one-yard line, 78 yards away from the line of scrimmage. Now the Seminoles were in position to cross the goal line and did with a field goal to win the game, 24–21. It was one of College Football's top all-time games.

Involving God in the entire process from discovering where He wants you to be, then getting in the proper position, making wise decisions, and using the talents he has given you will get you across that goal line no matter where you are starting from.

## Prayer for Guidance

Lord, it is a struggle to get across that goal line. Our financial blocking, our defensive good intentions, or strategic plan to follow your lead often breaks down. We end up punting—having to take a new route. Help us to discern when this is your will, like the path through the Wilderness you took the Israelites on, and when it is our failure to communicate with you and discern the best way to go. Thank you, Lord, for hearing our prayers.

Amen.

# Chapter Fifteen

# HALFTIME

> *I have fought a good fight.*
> *I have finished the race and I have remained faithful.*
> *And now the prize waits me.*
>
> **2 Timothy 4: 7,8**

**G**reat halftime talks are the stuff of legends. Your team has "dumbed around" all first half and you find yourself behind. You have to find a way to get that runaway train back on track.

The simplest way to accomplish that might be to quote a famous baseball player. After Yogi Berra had concluded his playing career he turned to managing. In 1973, his New York Mets team found itself nine games out of first place when a reporter asked him if his team was out of the pennant race. Yogi replied, "It ain't over 'til it's over."[44]

That's the first thing any coach wants his team to realize at halftime. The game is not over! It doesn't matter what they did in the first half, the game "ain't over" yet. If they are ahead, he stresses "don't let up." If they are behind, "don't give up."

Bobby Bowden has a standard bit of advice he springs on his team at the half if they are leading. "Men, in the second half, if they don't score, we win." Okay, so it is not rocket science, but it is a fact, and it never hurts to remind a group of 18 to 21-year-olds of the importance of continuing to play hard

And of course, all the miracle comebacks that have occurred in the second half of football games, where teams have "snatched victory from the jaws of certain defeat," provide grist for the halftime-talk-mill.

Coaches can always remind their players of the games mentioned earlier in this book, such as 1992 when Frank Reich led Buffalo to victory after trailing Houston by 32 points at the half (see Chapter Four: The Offense). Or they could refer to 1994 in Tallahassee when Danny Kanell (Chapter Three: The Quarterback) led Florida State to a tie over Florida after trailing by 28 points in the fourth quarter.

As far as a halftime pepper-upper given by someone other than a coach, October 23, 1999 would be a good one. Coach Bobby Bowden was going for his 300th career win on this night in Clemson, South Carolina. The 'Noles had an awful first half and trailed by 11 points, the biggest halftime deficit they had faced in five years. To lose would be doubly embarrassing because not only would their coach be deprived of his 300th win, he would lose to his son—Tommy Bowden, the Tigers' coach.

Strength coach Dave Van Halanger recreated the scene in the book *Florida State Faith*. Coach Van remembers how quiet the locker room was as senior noseguard Corey Simon walked to the middle of the room. "Basically Corey just challenged each player to stay in the locker room and not go back out if they weren't prepared to play the game of their lives in the second half. He let them know he intended to leave it all on the field."[45] With Simon leading the way, FSU shutout Clemson in the second half and scored two touchdowns to win 17–14.

**2 Timothy 4** is our "game ain't over" reminder. For unless we continue to fight a good fight every day and stay the course we won't be able to claim victory. When Paul gave these words of advice to Timothy, the apostle was near the end of his life. Paul could look back and say with confidence he had *fought the good fight, finished the race and remained faithful.* He was giving Timothy a little halftime talk to remind him that no matter how difficult the fight might seem to be, keep on fighting and when he was finally with Jesus Christ, he would discover it was all worth it.

In **Psalm 48** the Psalmist praises God for His protection and says in verses 11–14, *Let the towns of Judah be glad for your judgments are just. Go and inspect the city of Jerusalem. Walk around and count the many towers, take note of the fortified walls, and tour all the citadels that you may describe them to future generations. For that is what God is like. He is our God forever and ever and He will be our guide until we die.*

In other words, whether we are winning or losing, happy or sad, in times of joy or travail, we should continually inspect our defenses to make sure the foundations are strong. The foundations include faith, knowledge of the Bible, prayer, and fellowship with believers. Then praise Him for His protection.[46]

A coach may find it necessary to review the fundamentals of football at halftime. He may have to talk about blocking and tackling, pass protection, and play execution. All of these must be crisp in the second half to win.

One of the most famous and often quoted halftime speeches was given on November 10, 1928, at Yankee Stadium when Notre Dame and Army were locked in a scoreless battle. Knute Rockne, the combination coach, father-figure, and psychologist huddled his team around him and told them in the hushed dressing room the story of former Fighting Irish player George Gipp who had died eight years earlier of pneumonia.

Rockne told his players that he was going to tell them something he had not told anyone before. He revealed that Gipp had said to him, as he lay dying, " 'Someday, Rock, sometime when the going gets tough, when the odds are against us, ask the boys to win one for the Gipper.' Boys, those were his dying words. I've never repeated them before because they were meant for just one game. Men, this is that game." Notre Dame beat Army 12–6.

Rockne was the master of locker room emotion. Once he maintained total silence in the locker room for 20 minutes, then stood, looked at his team, and shouted, "Fight! Fight! Fight!" His team charged out and smeared Northwestern. Knute Rockne coached for 12 years in which he won 105 games against 12 losses and five ties. He was killed in a plane crash March 31, 1931, at the age of 43. Memories of his inspiring halftime talks live on.[47]

It doesn't matter if we are at halftime or in the final quarter. God looks for us to keep on fighting that good fight and running the entire race with dignity and honor, and our faithfulness will be rewarded when the game is over.

When a reporter questioned Yogi Berra in July of 1973 about his season being over and prompted his now infamous "ain't over 'til it's over" quote, Yogi knew what he was talking about. The Mets won the pennant.

## Prayer for Guidance

Lord, we realize how important it is to keep on fighting the good fight. We know when we let our defenses down we are susceptible to Satan's knockout punch. Remind us daily, Lord, that the "game ain't over til it's over" so we may be prepared for every challenge and at the end of the game may take home the prize You have for us. Thank You for hearing our prayers.

Amen!

## Chapter Sixteen

# SCOUTING THE OPPONENTS

*After exploring the land for forty days the men returned...*
*They reported to the people what they had seen...*
*It is indeed a magnificent country—a land flowing with*
*milk and honey. But, the people living there are powerful*
*and their cities are fortified...But, Caleb tried to encourage*
*the people as they stood before Moses. "Let's go at once*
*to take the land," he said. "We can certainly conquer it."*

Numbers 13: 25,27-28, 30

Chances are that guy up in the tree across the street from the practice field really is employed by a tree service to trim the branches. In the past he might have been a spy who was trying to steal some information to help your opponent. However, with the advent of video tape, computers, satellite dishes, fax machines, email, and a plethora of football games on television, coaches have access to a lot of information about their opponents. It isn't necessary to send a scout on a covert spying mission.

Oh sure, coaches still talk. They pass information back and forth. But scouting the opponents has become easier and more sophisticated. A team may still send someone to scout a future opponent at a stadium where your team will have to play on the road, but most of the decisions that show up in that game plan are gleaned from watching a video tape of the opponent.

Football coaching staffs spend countless hours scouting an opponent by looking at videos of them. It is a never-ending process. They study each play, formation, coverage, and defensive front from the previous three or four games—minimum. They'll study games from the last season and even previous games involving their head-to-head matchups.

Coaches are always looking for something to help give them an edge in a game. Sometimes, on tape, they may spot something an opposing player does to tip off a play. It could be the way a lineman positions his feet on a run as opposed to a pass play. Perhaps a quarterback only licks his fingertips before the snap on a passing play.

Scouting is a process of looking for strengths and weaknesses, then finding a way to overcome them. But a coaching staff does not want to spend an inordinate amount of time talking about the opponents' strengths. Better to show the players how they will attack an opponent rather than saying how good the opponent is in an area, thereby creating doubts in their own team's minds.

In the Old Testament book of **Numbers**, we learn that God had led the Israelites from Egypt to the brink of the Promised Land. There were 12 scouts sent by Moses, and they went on an assignment to check out the territory. Their journey took them about 500 miles round trip.

The report they gave said *We arrived in the land you sent us to see and it is indeed a magnificent country—a land flowing with milk and honey. Here is some of its fruit as proof.* Numbers 13:27 (NLT)

That was a pretty accurate scouting report. One that jibed with God's plan. Too bad they had an addendum. *But, the people living there are powerful and their cities and towns are fortified and very large. We also saw descendents of Anak living there.* Numbers 13: 28. It was that little "Anak" thing thrown in that colored their report. Anak was a tribe of people that is believed to be the group that Goliath was descended from. Some of their men were seven to nine feet tall.

Caleb tried to encourage the people saying, "He, we can take that land. We Bad! We the Dudes! Hey, God's on our side; they can't beat us." He wanted to go at once and overtake them using the element of surprise.

The other men who had explored the land now chimed in. *We can't go up against them. They are stronger than we are. So, they spread discouraging reports...The land will swallow up any who go to live there. All the people were huge...We felt like grasshoppers next to them and that's what we looked like to them.* Numbers 13: 31–33.

It took courage for Caleb to stand up to the other scouts and say they were wrong. The NLT says when we go against a crowd we must (1) have the facts; (2) have the right attitude; (3) state clearly what we believe.[48] Caleb did these things; therefore, he was eventually allowed to enter Canaan whereas all the rest of the adults (except Joshua) who had left Egypt never entered the Promised Land. Those people had been defeated by a scouting report that placed too much emphasis on the opponent's strength.

Satan is a strong opponent. Therefore we must be alert to what strategies he uses to deceive, confuse, and intimidate us. We know we have strength on our side, but sometimes we get involved in wrong-thinking and don't realize it until we have made a mistake. We need to scout out the courses available in advance and ask the Holy Spirit to guide us in taking the right path.

The Tennessee Titan defense faced a formidable task in trying to control the damage a high powered St. Louis Ram offense could do to them in Super Bowl XXXIV. They only had a week to prepare so time was of the essence in scouting the opponent. They chose to look at the tape of the Tampa Bay-St. Louis game in the playoffs. Although the Buccaneers lost, they held the high-scoring Ram offense to 11 points.

"One of the keys we came away with was making sure to minimize the yards after the catch," said Titan Defensive Coordinator Gregg Williams. "What Tampa Bay did against St. Louis, as well as anyone I've seen in years, is tackle extremely well." [49] Although the Titan defense played admirably in the Super Bowl, they lost 23–16.

Although your life has to be lived today, it never hurts to have advance information to assist in making decisions tomorrow. Bible study is an excellent scouting tool.

# Prayer for Guidance

Lord, we know that the territory has already been well-scouted for us. You know the best strategy for the past, present, and future. Help us to rely on your Word for instruction and the Holy Spirit for guidance that we may not be denied access to the Promised Land. We know you have a plan, and we ask for wisdom to know and fulfill our part in it.

Amen

## Chapter Seventeen

# THE FANS

*A huge crowd of Passover visitors took palm branches
and went down to the road to meet Him. They shouted,
"Praise God, bless the One who comes in the name of the Lord.
Hail to the King of Israel."*

*John 12: 12–13*

**"I**t was back last October, I believe it was. We was going
to hold a tent service off at one of them college towns,
and we got there about dinner time on Saturday."

Saturdays in the fall! There's nothing like 'em, unless it's
Sundays in the Fall. That's when the football fans are in their glory.
All over America, in small towns and big cities, football teams com-
pete in front of their fans. Ah yes, the fans. Some are well-informed
and some aren't. But, they all think they know how their team should
play the game.

*"We followed this whole raft of people...we commenced to go through all kinds of doors and gates and I looked up over one of 'em and it said, North Gate."*

The word fan is a shortened version of "fanatic" meaning "overly zealous." And that's what many fans are—out of control zealots. Just take a look at some of the camera shots in the stands on the next televised game you watch. Some of those get-ups are not your normal attire. You'll see people with cheese on their heads, hogs on their heads, or Viking helmets, and wearing all kinds of masks while decked out in outrageous attire. Fanatics.

Of course, the dictionary definition that fits most fans is: "a person enthusiastic about a specified sport."[50] Those whose team wins the game usually fit that description of a fan nicely. Those who lose more closely resemble fanatics in their actions.

*"Everybody got to where they was a-going because they parted and I could see pretty good. What I seen was this whole raft of people a-sittin' on these two banks lookin' at one another across this pretty little green cow pasture...Somebody had took and drawed white lines acrost it and drove posts in it and I don't know what all."*

Each fan has his own team that he or she lives and dies for each football weekend. When their team wins they are in hog heaven (especially if they are an Arkansas fan—pun intended). But, lose, and despondency descends on their side of the stadium. They turn surly. They don't want to talk or hear about the game.

*"I seen 30 or 40 men come running out of one end of a great big outhouse down there and everybody where I was a settin' got up and hollered."*

It is amazing how quickly things can change. People, being emotional human beings, can do a quick reversal when things aren't going the way they want them to. Jesus began his last week on earth as an adored hero. He had performed many miracles and done a lot of amazing things. The people figured that, at long last, God had sent them the King they had been longing for.

**John 12** describes his triumphant entry into Jerusalem. The crowds were huge, excited, and loud as they awaited His arrival. Then they saw Him coming, and the noise level got louder and louder. They broke off palm branches and held them up from both sides of the road to form a canopy for their King to ride through.

And there He came. The One they had heard about who had raised Lazarus from the dead. He was here. Riding on a donkey. The one the prophets had talked and written about. The King of Kings. The National Leader the Jews had been waiting for. It was a day of great excitement. A day of celebration!

One week later when He had been arrested these same people turned on Him, even though there was nothing with which He could legitimately be charged.  Pilate said in **John 18: 38–40 *He is not guilty of any crime. But, you have a custom of asking me to release someone from prison each year at Passover. So, if you want me to, I'll release the King of the Jews. No, they shouted back. No! Not this man, but Barabbas. (Barabbas was a criminal) NLT.*** Those who were His fans—in just one week—had turned on Jesus.

*"I seen that evenin' the awfulest fight that I ever have seen in all my life. They would run at one another and kick one another and throw one another down and stomp on one another and griiind their feet into one another and I don't know what-all and just as fast as one of 'em would get hurt, they'd take him off and run another one on."*

Football fans can be fickle. Make a good play and they cheer to their heart's content. Then when you make a mistake that costs you the game, the boo's come cascading down. Fair weather fans is a term that has sprung up to describe those fans who jump off the band wagon. Teams that make it all the way to the final game of the Super Bowl pick up a lot of new-found friends along the way. If they lose the Super Bowl, the wagon-load gets a lot lighter.

Even though only two teams out of all the ones playing football, can make it to the Championship Game, the one who gets there but doesn't win it is tabbed a loser. It is as if they never made it to the Big Game at all because of all the grief they catch over losing it once they got there.

*"I don't know, friends, to this day, what it was they was a-doin' down there, but I have studied about it. I think it is some kindly of a contest where they see which bunchful of them men can take that pumpkin and run from one end of that cow pasture to the other without gettin' knocked down or steppin' in somethin'."*

In life you are going to get knocked down, but the important thing is to get back up and do it better next time. The next time may be your special time. Former Alabama quarterback, coach, and administrator Steve Sloan pointed out that the "sun doesn't shine on the same dog everyday." [51] In other words, your day will come, and it will feel good to be on the top of the heap.

Keeping things in perspective, win or lose, is the main thing. Don Shula said, "Winning is not final."[52] And Jake Gaither pointed out we should "Expect to lose sometimes, but a loss can be a stepping stone to victory if it's utilized in the right way."[53] Don't be a fair-weather fan.

Andy Griffith posed as a country bumpkin and an unwitting fan in his 1950's recording of "What it was was Football"[54] that has been quoted throughout this devotion. He used that early role to go on to a long, successful acting career in movies and on television. He was a fan who was a winner in the end.

## Prayer for Guidance

Lord, help us to take setbacks and successes in stride. We know it is the way we handle this journey through life that is important. My we always be your fans in fair weather and through storms. We know how we want things to turn out. We trust you to lead us down the path of righteousness that leads to victory.

Amen

## Chapter Eighteen

# THE COLLEGE NATIONAL CHAMPIONSHIP

*For you made us only a little lower than God
and You crowned us with glory and honor.*

Psalm 8:5

**H**ow to determine a true National Champion for College Football? It's the question that still plagues NCAA Division 1-A football. For some reason it is not a problem with other major and minor sports, but the highest level of college football has had trouble figuring out how to do it.

In 1992 they formed the Bowl Coalition. In 1995 they changed and renamed it the Bowl Alliance. Then, in 1998, along came the Bowl Championship Series—the BCS. The BCS uses a combination of the AP and Coaches polls, computer polls, a team's strength of schedule, and credit for quality wins, to determine who the top two teams are. Then, those teams play for the National Championship in the designated Bowl Game. The Bowls that share hosting duties for the Big Game and have it every four years are: the Rose Bowl, Sugar Bowl, Orange Bowl, and Fiesta Bowl.

In his heart every player wants to play in the National Championship game. In each fan's heart there is a desire to have his or her team win the National Championship. There are multitudinous opinions concerning how to determine just who gets a chance to do this. Most people just can't understand what the problem is. Why is there a holdup in simply setting up a playoff to determine the real national champion. After all, 1-AA has been doing it for years. If Division 1-A can't figure this out, why don't they just look at what 1-AA is doing?

But, the powers that be in 1-A say it ain't that easy. College football and bowl games go way back. When you hear sportscaster Keith Jackson say the Rose Bowl is the "Granddaddy of the Bowl Games," you can recall this story and understand the special relationship that college football has with the bowls.

Back in 1901 some California folks decided the polo match played in conjunction with the Tournament of Roses Parade just wasn't getting it. So they decided to play a football game pitting the best of the East against the Best of the West. Stanford was the "Champion of the Pacific Coast Universities" and Michigan ruled the East.

The Wolverines accepted the invitation to play the game on January 1, 1902. They left Ann Arbor on December 17th with temperatures below freezing and six inches of snow on the ground. Eight days later, they were greeted with 80 degree weather in warm, sunny California.

8,000 fans showed up for what turned out to be not much of a game. The Wolverines, who had outscored opponents 501–0 in 10 games, crushed Stanford 49–0. In fact, with eight minutes remaining in the game, Stanford captain Ralph Fisher walked to the Michigan bench and offered to concede. The beasts of the east accepted the concession. Despite the fact that the Tournament of Roses made a profit of $3,161.86 on the game, they feared the blow-out had turned people off and didn't schedule another post-parade football game for 16 years.[56]

No matter what system is used to get to the big game, the teams must win those regular season games to qualify. To be good enough, the players must practice well. They must believe in themselves, their coaches, and their teammates. The competition is so tough that one slip during the season could keep them out of the championship game. There's little margin for error.

Likewise, we are on a journey to a final destination and it is important to practice well each day, to play well in the real game. The Lord has equipped us to do the job. In **Psalm 8:5** we are reminded that God has made us just a little lower than Himself. The *Believer's Bible Commentary* says, "God made man in His own image and after His own likeness. Though lower than God, man shares with Him some faculties that are not shared by any other order of creation on earth. Everything God made was pronounced to be good, but the verdict on the creation of man was 'very good.'"

If you get discouraged in some of the daily battles that threaten to consume you, think about this. God created a magnificent universe whose size is hard to comprehend. When you talk about distances in relation to the entire universe, they must be measured in light years—the distance light travels in a year. Since light moves at the speed of 186,000 miles per second and there are 31.5 million seconds in a year, then light travels roughly six trillion miles in a year.[55]

How astounding is that? God made all that and he made us. Not only that, He made us just a little lower than Himself.

God gave us authority over all the earth and the animals that roam it. We are higher than the fish of the deep, the reptiles, and the birds of the air. Sometimes these animals try to attack us, but he has given us the ability and the mental capacity to determine how to protect ourselves. Since we don't have to spend all our time worrying about how to defend ourselves against the rest of creation, God expects more of us than being "couch potatoes." **Lamentations 3: 22-23 says *Because of the Lord's great love we are not consumed, for His compassions never fail. They are new every morning; great is your faithfulness.*** So, every day presents itself as a brand new day unlike any that has come before it. We don't have to worry about light. God has taken care of that. We don't have to worry about the sun forgetting to go down to bring about the night. God has taken care of that.

King David told us the best way to handle the challenges of the day in **Psalm 5:3: *In the morning, O Lord you hear my voice; in the morning I lay my requests before you and wait in expectation.*** It's good to go to God first thing in the morning and ask for help that day.

Pop Warner was the first to say, "You play the way you practice."[57] So it is our daily lives that count. It's how we travel on this journey through life that is important. We take the right road, make the right decisions, and do the right things by consulting God. We are His representatives on earth. He made us only slightly lower than himself.

But, whether a playoff system is used to determine the participants or they stick with the current BCS system, some team will be crowned National Champions. As for all the rest of us, we have already been crowned. As it says in **Psalm 8:5**, we have been "crowned with glory and honor."

## Prayer for Guidance

Lord, may we approach each day as the champions you have already crowned us to be when you made us a little lower than you. May we wear this crown with honor and conduct ourselves daily as the champions you created us to be.

Amen

## Chapter Nineteen
# THE SUPER BOWL

*And Jabez called on the God of Israel saying, "Oh that you would bless me indeed, and enlarge my territory... So God granted him what he requested.*

Chronicles 4:9-10

**W**hen the late Bill Peterson took over the coaching reigns of the Houston Oilers, the first thing he did was call a team meeting. After all the players were assembled and curiously awaited the new coach's first words, Coach Pete said, "Men, this season I want you thinking about one word and one word only. That word is Super Bowl."[58]

With his usual propensity for mixing up his words, Coach Pete had miscounted his words, but he hadn't miscalculated their importance. The Super Bowl is simply the grandest, most spectacular of all sports events. It's the game every pro football team wants to be playing in while all the others have packed their bags and gone home for the winter. More hype surrounds it. More advertising dollars are spent on it. And more information is written, broadcast, videotaped, and televised about this one football game than any other.

Peter Boulware, outside linebacker for the Baltimore Ravens, described the extraordinary experience of jogging onto the playing field of Raymond James Stadium in Tampa for Super Bowl XXXV. Boulware was thinking, "Man, I am living a dream. As a kid you always dream of playing in this game, but you never really think you would get here. I looked around the stadium and realized, I was living that dream. It was an awesome experience, the greatest you'll ever have as a football player."[59]

The Super Bowl started as a grudge match between the long-established National Football League and the upstart American Football League. The two leagues were at war. They battled it out for top draft choices of college talent. Now they would meet on the gridiron on January 15, 1967, in the first Super Bowl.

The NFL champs Green Bay showed the new league they still had some improving to do to reach championship level. In Super Bowl I, the Packers smacked the Kansas City Chiefs, 35–10. Then they turned around and did the same thing to the Oakland Raiders in Super Bowl II, defeating Oakland 33–14.

But the real breakthrough came in Super Bowl III. The New York Jets had bested the NFL in the battle for signing rights to a slick quarterback out of Alabama by the name of Joe Namath. They won him over with an astronomical (at that time) offer of $400,000.

When the Jets played Baltimore in the Super Bowl, the brash, young Namath not only boldly predicted, but "guaranteed" a Jets' victory. The nerve of that guy thinking he could beat Don Shula, Johnny Unitas, and company! Namath's bold guarantee was as good as gold, as the Jets defeated the Colts 16–7 and he was named MVP.

In **1 Chronicles 4** we encounter another bold statement. The first four chapters of Chronicles have been a methodical genealogical history of the Jewish people. This list, name-by-name would run on for ten chapters. It was simply a dry, unadorned list of the descendents from Adam through Zerubbabel. Nothing is really said about any of these. Their names are simply listed.

Well, there was one exception. When he came to the name of Jabez, the writer, presumed to be Ezra, stopped the listing of names and made this statement *Jabez was more honorable than his brothers. His Mother had named him Jabez saying, "I gave birth to him in pain." Jabez cried out to the God of Israel , "Oh that you bless me and enlarge my territory. Let your hand be with me and keep me from harm, so I will be free from pain."* That was a pretty bold request. But, you know what? The end of **verse 10** states *And God granted his request.*

We are told to be bold, not timid, in our role as Christians. So, doing as Jabez did and asking God to be Lord over our work, time with our family, and our recreation is fine. It's what Jabez did and God answered his prayer.

Bruce Wilkinson has written a highly successful little book about these two verses of scripture on Jabez. His book, *The Prayer of Jabez,* has sold millions of copies.[60]

Wilkinson points out on page 43 that to pray for enlarged territory is to ask for a miracle. The good news is God is still in the miracle-working business. Many people in these contemporary times don't believe that God still works miracles. It would be hard for God to perform a miracle in their lives because of the unbelief.

Wilkinson said he started praying the prayer of Jabez 30 years ago and hasn't stopped. The key is in the believing. I've heard people, even some ministers, scoff at the idea of praying this prayer and getting anything out of it. But Wilkinson, whose *Walk thru the Bible* ministries has provided Biblical teaching and training tools for hundreds of thousands says, "If you were to ask me what sentence, other than my prayer for salvation, has revolutionized my life and ministry the most I would tell you it was…The prayer of Jabez."

Praying boldly in God's will and believing those prayers will be answered is the way to achieve victory in our lives. Just like Joe Namath fully believed he could deliver on that guarantee he made, and he did it. We must believe God will answer the prayer of Jabez or any prayer we pray in His will, then have faith those prayers will be answered.

Everything was coming up roses for the Miami Dolphins in 1972. They had a perfect record going into the Super Bowl—16 wins and no losses. Then they played virtually a perfect half of football in the first half of Super Bowl VII as they only allowed George Allen's Washington Redskins to cross mid-field twice. Playing with continuous good field position, they were able to score two touchdowns and led 14–0.

As it got later and later in the game it appeared that the Dolphins were not only going to finish with a perfect record, they would do it in style by shutting out the Redskins. Then, with 2:07 left in the game, perfection ended. The Dolphins misplayed the snap on an attempted field goal. In panic mode, Garo Yepremian grabbed the ball off the ground and attempted to pass it; something he had never tried before.

Well, lack of practice makes for lack of perfection and Garo proved it. His pitiful pass was picked off by the Redskins Mike Bass, who easily outran Garo for a 49-yard score. Now the Dolphins no longer were thinking shutout, the doubts crept in as to if they would even win the game, but they tenaciously clung to their dream and closed out the game a 14–7 winner. They are still the only NFL team to ever have a perfect season.

Jesus led the perfect life, but thank goodness He doesn't require us to be perfect. Through His life He has simply shown us a more excellent way to conduct our lives. And a guy named Jabez has shown us it is all right to boldly approach God in our prayers so we may not just settle for the playoffs, but aim for the Super Bowl in our lives.

## Prayer for Guidance

Lord, help us to approach each day as preparation for our own personal Super Bowl in life. May we recognize that each day is precious and the things we do are important. Thank you for the prayer of Jabez and the assurance it brings us, that we can boldly approach you with our requests, believing You will answer them and knowing no problem is too big or small for You. Give us the wisdom to seek the right things when we approach you and the boldness to carry out the actions you instruct us to take.

Amen

## Chapter Twenty

# GAME OVER

> *I have fought the good fight, I have finished the race and I have remained faithful. And now the prize awaits me—the crown of righteousness that the Lord, the righteous Judge, will give me on that great day of his return*
>
> **2 Timothy 4:7-8**

On September 13, 2003, Florida State played host to Georgia Tech. The Seminoles were favored by over three touchdowns. The Yellow Jackets would be starting a freshman quarterback and had lost quite a few players in the off-season. The Seminoles had not lost a Saturday night game in Tallahassee since 1989. It looked like a sure thing.

Then the home team got a rude surprise. The Jackets' defense shut down everything FSU tried and after one quarter the game was scoreless. Then Georgia Tech kicked a couple of field goals and as the teams went in at half time it was 6–0 in favor of the visitors. Bobby Bowden wasn't even able to use his favorite half-time talk, "Men if they don't score in the second half, we win" (see Chapter 15). Since the Seminoles were behind, he'd had to come up with another approach.

The home folks started getting restless when the Seminoles were still scoreless after three quarters. Three minutes into the fourth quarter FSU had finally made it down to the Tech "red zone" (inside the 20 yard-line) when Tech intercepted a pass in the end zone and returned it to mid-field. Two plays later, on a 47-yard touchdown run, the Yellow Jackets led the Seminoles 13–0.

Even though it was only the third game of the season, the Seminoles could see the national championship "handwriting on the wall." It read, "Lose this one and you're done." So they tightened their chin straps and started a drive. They scored to cut the lead to 13–7, but the drive had taken 12 plays and five precious minutes. Time was becoming the enemy. But, they got the ball again and scored in six plays to finally take the lead, 14–13.

Georgia Tech was not finished! After an interception, they began another drive. It was deathly quiet in the press box—not a word being spoken. Out in the stands the fans were on their feet, loudly yelling and trying to distract a Tech offense that continued to move downfield. Then it happened. The Seminole defense, which had been superb all night, intercepted a pass and a huge collective sigh of relief escaped the stadium.

After I filed my final ESPN radio report I noticed, for the first time, my shoulders ached, muscles were tight, and my fingers tingled. Such is the fallout when a tough game is over. The headlines in the *Tallahassee Democrat* on Sunday morning read: "Die Another Day."

Football is not life or death. Sometimes it just seems like it. Rabid fans will tell you there is no feeling much worse than losing to your arch rivals. FSU vs Florida; Georgia vs Georgia Tech;

Alabama-Auburn; Michigan-Michigan State; Army-Navy; Southern Cal-UCLA; Texas-Texas A&M; Washington-Washington State. The losing team in those games suffers cruel and unusual punishment because they have to live with the outcome for an entire year.

When the apostle Paul was nearing the end of his life, he gave these words of encouragement to Timothy: *I have fought the good fight. I have finished the race. I have remained faithful and now the prize awaits me.* Timothy was a young man who Paul had chosen to accompany him on some of his missionary journeys. Timothy was, by nature, timid and reserved. Paul was the opposite. But he saw great potential in Timothy, who was the recipient of two letters from Paul that are now New Testament books.

As Paul looked back on his life he remembered how he had been bitten by a snake, shipwrecked, threatened, imprisoned, and punished for his preaching of the gospel of Jesus Christ. Yet, he persevered. Now he was offering these life experiences as words of encouragement for all of us. We are advised to fight the good fight, run the race to the finish, and to remain faithful to the finish. But nowhere does it say any game is, in itself, as important as life and death.

The Seminoles had gotten close to a national championship on a number of occasions, but not until 1993, their 47th year of playing football and their 18th season under Bobby Bowden, did they win it. But Coach Bowden was able to keep all of that in proper perspective and not be devastated by the pressure of not winning it all. He cites **Matthew 16:26** as his guiding influence. *For what profit is it to a man if he gains the whole world and loses his own soul.* Coach Bowden will not sell out to win a football game—even the national championship game.

In his book *More than just a Game* Bobby says, "You know there are some folks who actually hate other folks over football. I'm always amazed there is so much hate in the world. Some fans are just awful. They act like they actually hate the other team. They take it too seriously. It's just a game."[61]

We could all stand to do some reflecting on Bobby's words. Football is just a game says the man who lives it day in and day out. So why can't we as fans and supporters of a team put it in proper perspective...no matter if we win or lose?

Eddie Robinson, Grambling's remarkable coach who won 408 games and only lost 165 summed it up for all coaches, players, and fans when he gave these words of wisdom. "Win without braggin'. Lose without acting the fool!"[62]

Thanks, coach! Game Over!

## Prayer for Guidance

Lord, we thank you for the game of football. It's a wonderful sport that gives us many, many hours of entertainment. Help us to enjoy the game and to accept each outcome graciously in grateful appreciation for the freedom to watch, cheer, and enjoy it. Keep the fun in and the hate out of football, we pray.

Amen.

# AFTERWORD

**F**ootball is a wonderful game. It can be very complex and difficult to figure out if you get lost in the X's and O's of the playbook. It can be very frustrating if your team and your favorite players do not perform like you want them to. Cheering your team on, only to meet defeat, can be disappointing, frustrating, and anger inducing—if you let it.

Don't let it! Football is still a game played with the same funny, oblong-shaped ball we kicked around as kids. It is still coached and played by imperfect human beings.

God has greatly blessed the game of football. He has enabled this game to become an enormously popular form of entertainment. He has allowed football to evolve into a profitable big business. The game of football now reaches and influences many areas of our society. Many football players have become leaders in business, the military, government, entertainment, and religion.

God did not intend for football to become our god. It is still just a game. Throw a football into the air and let it hit the ground. You cannot predict which way this odd-shaped ball with bounce. Likewise, life can take some funny bounces, some that lead you along paths you could not have predicted or ever expected.

The One who controls all the funny bounces in life controls football, too. So, we should enjoy each game for its fun, excitement, suspense, and outcome. Then thank God for the game of football. Bobby Bowden says, "I have never gone through a single day without a blessing from God."

Football is a blessing to be enjoyed!

*—Jim*

# ABOUT THE AUTHOR

**J**im Crosby has been a football fan all his life. Born in Macon, Georgia during the Charley Trippi-led Georgia Bulldog years, he moved to the Sunshine State and graduated from Florida State University. He has seen every Florida State football game since 1957 and covered the two national championships the Seminoles won under Bobby Bowden. While living in Fort Lauderdale, he followed the Miami Dolphins from their beginning through their improbable perfect season in 1972 to today.

Now residing in Tallahassee, Florida, he reports on football for ESPN Radio and broadcasts Seminole baseball games while working for Clear Channel Worldwide. He writes books, articles, and is a frequent public speaker in churches and civic groups. Jim's first book, *Monday Morning Devotions,* was published in November 2002. He is currently working on two new books scheduled for completion in 2004.

Jim enjoys studying the Bible, reading good fiction, walking on the beach and in the mountains, and doing anything with his wife, Susette.

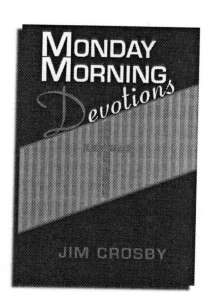

## MONDAY MORNING DEVOTIONS

If you enjoyed *Devotions for the Armchair Quarterback* check out this book by Jim Crosby available at amazon.com.

*Monday Morning Devotions* will jump-start your week in a positive, faith-affirming manner. In the book, author Jim Crosby has assembled quotes, stories, topics, scriptures, and prayers previously shared with his devotional group at work. These weekly motivational messages address workplace problems, family difficulties, individual struggles and spiritual hurdles. They are designed to help the reader apply Christian principles at work and other areas of life. *Monday Morning Devotions* is not just about problems. Within these pages you'll find that joy and humor abounds. Topics such as "God Nods," "If God is in Control Why Can't I get My Car Started," and "Another Bowl of Soup" are easily recalled, applied to daily living, and shared with others. Each self-contained lesson may be read in 10 minutes or less. The devotions can be used to start a Monday morning devotional group at work, shared in Bible study groups, or enjoyed at home. These 52 non-denominational devotions help the reader take the kinds of lessons learned on Sunday in church to work on Monday. *Monday Morning Devotions* will make Mondays better and enrich your entire week.

# BIBLIOGRAPHY

[1] *Winning,* compiled and edited by Michael Lynberg, Doubleday, New York, 1993, 117.

[2] *"All Things Possible."* Kurt Warner with Michael Silver, Harper and Zondervan, 2000, intro.

[3] *"All Things Possible."* ibid, 256.

[4] *"The Prayer of Jabez,* by Bruce Wilkinson with David Kipp, Multnomah Publishers, Sisters, Oregon, 2000.

[5] "Prayer Motives," edited by Dave Branon, *Sports Devotional Bible,"* Zondervan, Grand Rapids, Michigan, 2002, p. 1449.

[6] *Everyone's a Coach,* by Don Shula and Ken Blanchard, Harper Business, New York and Zondervan, Grand Rapids, MI, 1995, pp. 45–46.

[7] *Fourth and One,* by Joe Gibbs with Jerry Jenkins, Thomas Nelson Publishers, Nashville, 1991, p. 263.

[8] *Florida State Faith,* by Jim Crosby, projected publication date, December 2004.

[9] *Miracle in Miami,* by Lou Sahadi, Henry Regnery Company, Chicago, 1972, pp. 181–2.

[10] *The Wisdom of Southern Football,* compiled and edited by Criswell Freeman, Walnut Grove Press, Nashville, TN, 1995, p. 94.

[11] *Winning,* p. 5.

[12] *The Wisdom of Southern Football,* p.40.

[13] *Super Boulware* by Jim Crosby in Sports Spectrum, Sept–Oct, 2001, 16-21.

[14] *The First Fifty Years: The Story of the National Football League,* prepared and produced by the Creative Staff of NFL Properties, Inc, the Benjamin Company (Simon&Schuster Inc.) New York, 1969, pp.111, 221.

[15] *Winning ,* p. 41.

[16] *The Purpose Driven Life* by Rick Warren, Zondervan, Grand Rapids, MI, 2002, 211.

[17] *Wild at Heart,* by John Eldredge, Thomas Nelson Publishers, Nashville, 2001.

[18] *Wild at Heart,* p. 167.

[19] www. *chicagobears.com/tradition,* internet site, 2003

[20] *The Wisdom of Southern Football*, p. 34.

[22] *ESPN.com, Larry Schwartz*, 2003.

[23] *Life Application Study Bible, NLT*, Tyndale House Publishers, Inc., Wheaton, IL, 1996, p. 1549.

[24] Ghost*Riders in the sky, written by Stan Jones*, 1949.

[25] www.*Ramsusa.com*, LA Rams Fearsome Foursome, 2003.

[26] *Believer's Bible Commentary*, William Macdonald, Thomas Nelson Publishers, Nashville,1995, p. 1952.

[27] *www.glassweb.com, (Champions for Life web site)*, 2003.

[28] *www.nflplayers.com*, John Hannah, Larger than Life, by Jonathan Finkel, 2003.

[29] *www.southendzone.com/packer*, The 1967 NFL Championship, The Ice Bowl, Scott Crevier, 2003.

[30] *Life Application Bible, New Living Translation*,Tyndale House Publishers, Inc., Wheaton, IL, p. 838.

[31] *Life Application Bible*, ibid. p. 68 (comments).

[32] *detroitlions.com*, A look back: Dick "Night Train" Lane, 2003.

[33] *www.northcanton.sparcc.org* Browns legend leaves mark, Carl Morrison, 2003

[34] Talk by John Riley to Killearn United Methodist Men, Tallahassee, FL, 1995.

[36] *www.hickoksports.com*, Blanda, George F., Football, Sports Biographies, 2003.

[37] *Heart, Damn Yankees,*

[38] *Winning*, p. 43.

[39] *George Allen's Guide to Special Teams*, George Allen and Joe Pacelli, Human Kinetics Pub, June 1994, 227 pages.

[40] *Wild at Heart*, pp.141–2.

[41] *Wild at Heart*, pp 22–23.

[42] *Waking the Dead*, John Eldredge, Thomas Nelson Publishers, Nashville, 2003, p. 45.

[43] *www.philly.com* Mike Bruton, Inquirer Columnist, posted August 21, 2003.

[44] *The Yogi Book*, Yogi Berra, Workman Publishing, New York, 1998, p. 121.

[46] *Life Application Bible, New Living Translation*, p. 873.

[47] *The Augusta Chronicle On-line*, Rockne was master of locker-room emotion, by Mike Berardino, posted September 6, 1997.

[48] *Life Application Bible, New Living Translation*, p. 219.

[49] *www.superbowl.com*, Scouts leave no stone unturned, by Vic Carucci, reprinted from Super Bowl XXXVI program.

[50] *New Webster's World Dictionary, Third College Edition*, copyright 1991, p. 490.

[51] *The Wisdom of Southern Football*, p. 92.

[52] *The Wisdom of Southern Football*, p. 76.

[53] *The Wisdom of Southern Football*, p. 81.

[54] www.ziggazoomba.com/whatitwaswasfootball.php. September 10, 2003.

[55] *The Believer's Bible Commentary*, William MacDonald, Thomas Nelson Publishers, Nashville, 1995, p. 557.

[56] *www.umich.edu*, 1902 Rose Bowl.

[57] *Winning*, p. 41.

[58] *You can't become a football overnight*, by Jim Crosby, to be published in 2004.

[59] *Super Boulware* by Jim Crosby in *Sports Spectrum*, Sept–Oct, 2001, 16–21.

[60] *The Prayer of Jabez*, Bruce Wilkinson, Multnomah Publishers, Inc, Sisters, Oregon, 2000.

[61] *More than Just a Game*, Bobby Bowden with Bill Smith, Thomas Nelson Publishers, Nashville, 1994, p. 136.

[62] *The Wisdom of Southern Football*, p. 34.

The scriptures quoted in this book came from these three Bibles:

*Life Application Study Bible, New Living Translation*, Tyndale House Publishers, Inc., Wheaton, Illinois, 1996.

*Sports Devotional Bible, New International Version*, Dave Branon, General Editor, Zondervan, Grand Rapids, Michigan, 2002.

*The New Scofield Reference Bible, authorized King James Version*, New York, 1967.

Printed in the United States
21957LVS00001B/19-68